BALLOONOLOGY

BALLOONOLOGY

32 fun projects to take you from beginner to expert

JEREMY TELFORD

Photographs by Zac Williams

GIBBS SMITH

For my brother-in-law Paco, who introduced me to two of my greatest loves, my wife and balloons.

First Edition
14 13 12 11 10   5 4 3 2 1

Text © 2010 Jeremy Telford
Photographs © 2010 Zac Williams

Published by
Gibbs Smith
P.O. Box 667
Layton, Utah 84041

1.800.835.4993 orders
www.gibbs-smith.com

Designed by Dawn DeVries Sokol
Printed and bound in HongKong
Gibbs Smith books are printed on either recycled, 100% post-consumer waste, FSC-certified papers or on paper produced from a 100% certified sustainable forest/controlled wood source.

Library of Congress Cataloging-in-Publication Data

Telford, Jeremy.
  Balloonology : 32 fun projects to take you from beginner to expert / Jeremy Telford ; photographs by Zac Williams. — 1st ed.
     p. cm.
  ISBN-13: 978-1-4236-0745-8
  ISBN-10: 1-4236-0745-7
  1. Balloon sculpture. 2. Balloon decorations I. Title.
  TT926.T45 2010
  745.594—dc22
                           2010001324

Contents

Acknowledgments

I wish I knew who exactly to thank for my current ability in balloons. My education has come from so many sources over the years that I am sure it would be fairly impossible to thank all the people who have influenced me. There are names in the industry that have crossed my path more than once: Marvin Hardy, Ralph Dewey, and Larry Moss are just a few. But as big an influence as they are in the ballooning community they are a but a very small part of my education. So I guess I would have to thank the balloon twisting community as a whole. It is because of your willingness to share and to teach that I too am able to share and teach others now.

I do, however, know who to thank for the fact that this book has come together as beautifully as it has. It is in large part thanks to my editor, Lisa Anderson at Gibbs Smith, Publisher, that this book is even intelligible, and adding to that the great photography by Zac Williams has made this book one that I am very proud to share with you now.

Introduction

"Papa," said Jack, "can't you make me a balloon with this piece of whale entrail?"
—*The Swiss Family Robinson* (1813)

Balloons and balloon animals have an interesting history. The first balloons were made from animal bladders and intestines. I can't imagine they were very popular at that time, even if the entrails were cleaned really, really well. Putting my mouth on any kind of entrail is too much to ask for my art. I would rather be an accountant (sorry, Dad).

Luckily for us we now have nice, sterile, factory-made balloons to work with—they just *look* like intestines and bladders. It was years after this sanitary breakthrough that the first books on balloon sculpting came into being. For their time, these were innovative and creative books. They introduced to the world what balloon animals were supposed to look like. Most animals in the balloon world at the time resembled a dog with its legs stuck together. Some had longer necks and were called giraffes; others had short legs and a long tail and were called mice. Balloon animals have evolved since then. There are hundreds of beautifully rendered designs out there by as many balloon twisters. This is an art that continues to grow, mostly under the radar, but every now and then it pokes its head up and lets the public know how far it has advanced.

The books, too, have advanced. You can now find books that teach hundreds of different designs and hundreds of popular characters. They teach how to entertain and how to make money. In all there are thousands upon thousands of ways to use those little latex tubes. What we don't seem to have are books whose aim it is to teach people how to create their own designs. I'm sure most have heard the Chinese proverb: Give a man a fish and you feed him for a day. Teach a man to fish and you feed him for a lifetime. What the proverb neglects to mention is how much easier it is to give that fish than to teach someone the ins and outs of fishing. This is why so many of the various how-to books choose to hand out the fish. Cookbooks rarely teach how to cook or create your own dishes—they give you step-by-step recipes to follow. Many how-to art books teach you how to draw popular characters, not how to create your own. It is so much easier to give step-by-step instructions and leave it at that. In this particular case I don't think it is done out of greed. The balloon twisting community has always been open and sharing to those who want to learn. I'm sure all authors wish to sell their books, but these same people would stop and show you freely how to do a design if you ran into them on the street (unless you were in your car at the time, and even then some of them would still show you on the way to the hospital).

It is in that spirit, the spirit of sharing and . . . um . . . fishing, that this book was written. While this book contains over thirty uniquely different designs, it has much more than that. It is the purpose of this book to help you understand how, and to inspire you, to create your own designs. This is when balloon twisting really becomes fun. So you could say that this book has an infinite number of designs—just as soon as you figure them out. That's when you'll truly start fishing for yourself. (I might be overusing that fish analogy. It's starting to stink.)

If you are new to the balloon arts then I suggest you start from the beginning of the book. Learn the best way to inflate the balloon, how to tie it, and where to start twisting. When you get to the projects, it is especially important that you create them in the order they are presented in the book. Each design builds on the previous one, so creating them in order will ensure you have learned all the twists and techniques you'll need to know for the next design. And be sure to make every design in the book—you'll learn a little something from each one. By the time you've finished all the designs, you'll be amazed at how much you know! Then you can feel free to start playing and inventing on your own.

I placed the information you should eventually know, but that is especially boring to the beginner, at the back of the book so you don't have to read it right away. These are topics like how and where to store your balloons, the best balloon accessories, where to get a balloon apron, etc. This is stuff you should know just as soon as you feel like getting to it. I would suggest eventually getting to it.

All in all I've tried to make this book be as informative and entertaining as any book published on the subject. Well, actually I've tried to make it more informative and more entertaining, otherwise you might as well just buy that other book.

Now let's start twisting!

Before You Begin

Much of the following information can be found in greater detail toward the back of the book. Yet all of the following are things you need to know before you actually start twisting a sculpture—the bare bones of balloon twisting, if you will. If you have been twisting for any length of time you may already know some or all of it. If you do, please skip it—I will never know that you glossed over my witty comments and insightful explanations.

The pictures in this book are here so that you can see what the twister is doing for each project. I am not holding the balloons how I would normally hold them to create the designs comfortably or quickly. Don't try to force yourself and contort your arms and hands to the pictured positions—twist however is comfortable to you and I'll give out pointers periodically on the easiest ways to hold those little latex tubes. Also, my dominant twisting hand may be different than yours. If I say "right hand" but it seems more comfortable in your left, then switch those directions around too.

Balloons and Popping

Your balloons will pop. They will do it more when you are first starting, but even should you become a balloon-tying grandmaster, a few will still pop. Sometimes a bag of balloons will be from a batch that didn't turn out quite right or had been left out in the sun. Maybe one or two balloons had defects. Perhaps a child or younger sibling got to your design before you finished. The point is that it will happen, even if you do everything right. Don't be surprised when it does and try not to let yourself get too frustrated.

Children and Balloons

Very, very few people are injured by balloons each year (and those are mostly due to those pesky round helium balloons). That being said, balloons can still be a choking hazard. If you suspect that a child might put the balloon in his or her mouth, then don't risk it—no child's health is worth the risk. I find that by the time they are three years of age, most children have learned not to do so, but it's best to just ask the parent of the child. That way you remind the parent that the balloon can be a choking hazard while at the same time finding out if the child is beyond that stage. On the other hand, you can feel good knowing that balloons themselves are relatively "green." The recommended brands are made from tree sap, a renewable resource, and they are biodegradable and 100 percent nontoxic. (That still doesn't mean it's okay for children to try to eat them!)

Buying Balloons

Speaking of recommended brands, I suggest you get yourself a bag or two of assorted colors of either Qualatex or Betallatex balloons. Your local party store or an online balloon supplier will most likely carry one of these brands. If you buy them online, make sure you get a bag or two of size 260, a bag of 160, and a bag of 5" hearts. If you get them from a party store, size 260 is often the only size they carry. (If you can't get 160s or hearts at this time, just replace the 160 with a 260 in the directions of the design. I also give instructions so that you may use a 260 in place of the heart balloon.)

Inflating the Balloon

This is an important step unless you are making a dead worm. Dead worms require no inflation—in fact, they require no twisting or tying either. Dead worms come straight out of the bag, no assembly required. If you hope to make anything else, though, we should probably get some air into those balloons. There are two basic methods for doing so. You can put the balloon up to your mouth and blow—though I don't like this method because more often than not the blower faints or ruptures something—or you can use a pump. If you really, really want to blow the balloon with

your mouth and hope to do so without permanent damage to your body, try reading the guide in the back of the book (where I try to convince you not to a few more times). If you decided on sanity and consciousness, we'll teach you here how to use a pump. Realize that not all pumps are created equal. While at the party store or online, try to find a pump that has ridges on the cylindrical portion of it. This style of pump lasts a long time.

Using a Pump

I am going to assume you have a hand pump. If you have a motorized pump, the procedure is much the same except you don't apply effort, which ironically is what those crazy mouth blowers say about hand pumpers. One hand will grasp the cylindrical portion of the pump while the other hand guides the balloon onto the nozzle. With your pointer finger and thumb, roll the lip of the balloon over the nozzle, then pinch the balloon against the nozzle to hold it in place. Next pump that pump, making sure that you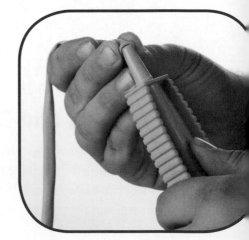

leave at least a couple of inches of uninflated balloon on the far, non-lipped end. The actual amount of uninflated balloon can vary depending on which design you are hoping to make, but unless otherwise stated, 2" or 3" will do. To remove the balloon, continue to apply pressure between your thumb and pointer finger and pull the balloon off. As the balloon comes off the pump, you should be pinching the balloon end and preventing the balloon from flying around the room and poking someone's eye. Then, unless you want to let go of the balloon and poke a few eyes (not recommended), or want to stand there for all eternity looking like a sculpture of the Greek god of balloon twisting (I believe his name was Inphlatewithease), you need to tie the end of that balloon.

Tying the Balloon

First you need to judge how much balloon you have available to tie your knot. Do you think you could tie a knot comfortably and easily with what you have pinched? If not, try one of these two methods: If the balloon is mostly inflated, use your free hand (go ahead and put down that pump) to pinch the balloon about

1" up from your other hand. Let that inch deflate by letting go with the hand that was holding the end. If the balloon is only inflated a few inches, it is often easier to squeeze the air a little toward the uninflated end until you have enough balloon to tie with. To tie the knot, pinch right below the bubble so the air doesn't escape. With your free hand, grab the end of the balloon. With the hand that is pinching the balloon, add your middle finger to that pinch so that your thumb is pinching the balloon between your pointer and middle fingers. The hand that is holding the end of the balloon should wrap it completely around the pointer and middle fingers of the pinching hand, ending so that the lip of the balloon crosses over the wrapped part and ends near the thumb. Use the thumb on the pinching hand to push the lipped end of the balloon between the pointer and middle fingers and under the wrapped part. My wife actually pushes with her non-pinching-hand thumb. Again, do what is comfortable. With your free hand, grab the end of the balloon and roll off the wrapped part while pulling it tight. Voilà—a tied balloon. Now you can do dead *and* live worms. You've doubled your repertoire!

Where to Start Twisting

We have one more important thing to teach before you begin twisting. With which end do you start twisting? It does matter. With extremely rare exceptions, you always twist from the side that has the knot and twist toward the side where you left that little bit uninflated. This is because as you twist the balloon into shapes, each twist pushes a small amount of air. If you start on the knotted side, the air begins to fill up the uninflated portion. If you start twisting from the other side, the air will make the balloon tighter and tighter until . . . well, let's just say this is how balloon phobias get started.

You now have the tools to get started (I mean beyond the two worm designs you've learned so far). What we need to do now is help get you comfortable with the basics of balloons, and teach you some of the more common twists. You are only moments from

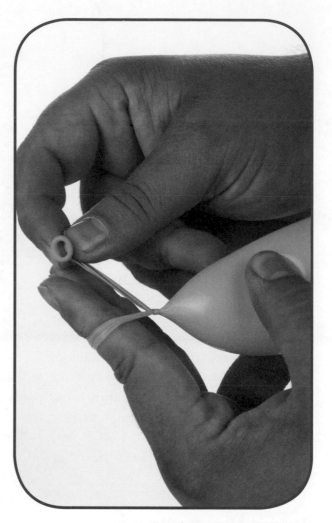

learning yet another design—the snake! I know what you're thinking, but I promise, it's better than that. But first, let's talk about putting twists in balloons.

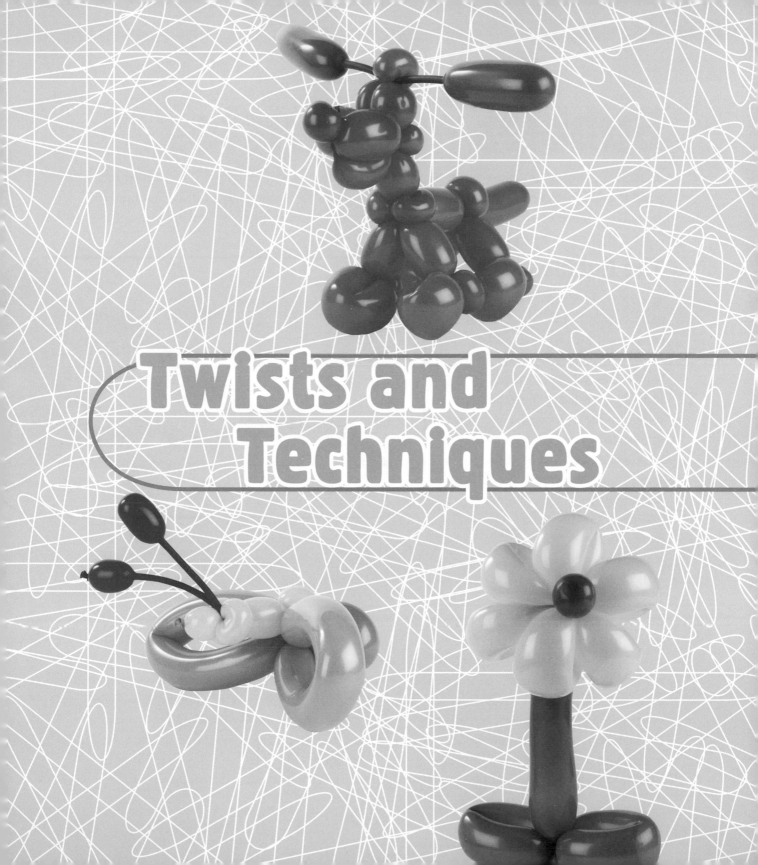

Twists and Techniques

Bubbles and Twists

All balloon twisting, simplified to the most basic of descriptions, consists of twisting bubbles into a balloon and then preventing them from becoming untwisted. Sounds easy, huh? In the end there are only a few real twists to teach, and most of those are just variations on three main principles:

The Bubble

The bubble is formed between any two twisted or uninflated parts of a balloon. When a balloon is first inflated it consists of one bubble from the knot to where the balloon is no longer inflated. When we put a twist into the balloon we create two bubbles, one from the knot to the twist, and the second from the twist to the uninflated part of the balloon. The problem with twisting simple bubbles is that they don't stay twisted by themselves. But we'll tackle that problem shortly.

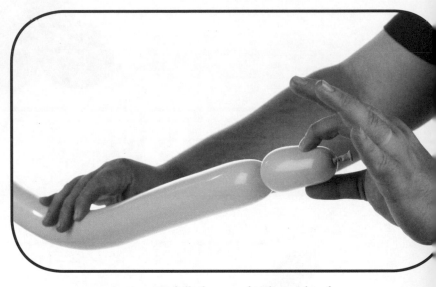

Let's try our first bubble (I mean beyond just inflating the balloon). Take an inflated balloon, and starting from the knot, measure up the balloon about 3". Put each hand on either side of the 3" mark (the left hand on the side closer to the knot), squeeze slightly with your left hand and then, while rolling your right hand forward, squeeze the balloon between the edge of your pointer finger and thumb on your right hand to make the twist. You may reset your right hand to twist more, just never fully let go of either side of the twist. Hopefully you've created a bubble. If you did it right it should look like the picture above (with the exception of perhaps a different color balloon). If you let go of either side of the bubble at this point the twist will come undone. This is because the balloon doesn't have anything to stop it from coming untwisted. I'm sure it can all be explained with one of Newton's laws or something. Basically you just need to remember that until a bubble (or series of bubbles) is twisted back into the balloon itself, it will come undone if you let it go. I know you've probably become attached to your little bubble, maybe even given it a pet name, but at this point it is time to let go. Don't worry, though, we'll let you make a new permanent bubble in just a second.

If I were to ask you to make this 3" bubble in a design, I would simply label it as this: **3" bubble.**

The Fold Twist

A fold twist is created whenever both ends of a single bubble are twisted into each other. The name "fold twist" refers to the whole thing—the bubble and the way it is twisted, not just to the small place where the balloon is twisted back into itself. If the bubble is very small, we call it a bear ear or pinch twist. If it is larger but you can't see through the middle of the fold, we just call it a fold twist. If the fold is so long that you can see through the middle, it is then called a loop.

Let's try a simple fold twist. From the knotted end of the balloon measure up about 3" and twist like we learned with the bubble. Hold that twist in place with one hand—cover the twist with the palm of one hand and curve your fingers around the twist. Both sides of the twist should be completely covered by the hand. Then move up another 5" and create another twist. Fold the bubble in half so the

two twists are next to each other. Now twist the two twists together. A good habit to learn is to roll your twist in. This is done by rotating, or rolling, one end of the balloon, usually the end that still has some uninflated balloon. Roll it away from you as you twist the two twists together. In this way the two twists will pull toward each other and this lessens the chance of an awkward pop. You can let go and it should stay. Again, it should look like the picture when finished.

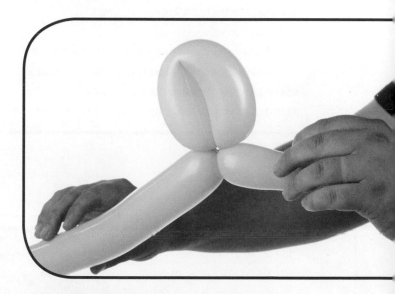

If I were to ask you to make the twist we just did in a design, I would label it like this:

3" bubble, 5" fold twist.

The Multi-Twist

The multi-twist is much like the fold twist, but the difference is that we make more than one bubble between the two twists that twist the balloon back into itself. The name "multi-twist" refers to all the bubbles and twists in the balloon between the two twists that are eventually twisted together. It does not refer solely to the point where the balloon is twisted back into itself. The number of bubbles you can have before twisting a balloon back into itself depends only on how much you have inflated the balloon and your dexterity in holding the balloon.

Let's try a simple multi-twist. From the knotted end of the balloon measure up 3" and make a twist, measure up another 3" and make another twist, measure up yet another 3" and

make a twist. Fold at the middle twist and twist the first and last twists together, remembering to roll in the segment of balloon with the uninflated portion into the twist. This is a multi-twist with two bubbles. A lot of people use this twist to make a pair of legs. Wondering if you did it right? Take a look at the picture.

If I were to ask you to make this twist, I would label it like this:

3" bubble, 3" x 3" multi-twist

These and variations on these are what many of the first designs are intended to teach. These in combination with a few other basic techniques will give you access to most of the balloon twisting skills used today. By the time you've finished the first section, you should even be able to try to create some designs of your own.

Okay, let's see if we can use those twists we learned in the context of a design. I will explain the twists again as we go through the creating process. Remember to look at the pictures often to see if your design looks like mine. If it doesn't, don't panic. See if simply rotating the twists around will do the trick. In fact there may come a time when yours doesn't look like mine on purpose.

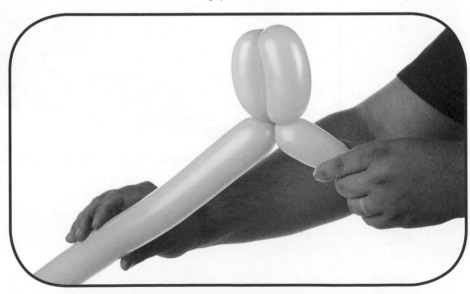

The Snake

The snake design is simple, quick, and one I still use today. It is a good place to get started, since balloons are like anything else worth doing—first you have to learn the basics really well and then you get to do the fun and flashy stuff. Here are the twists and techniques you will be learning (or reviewing): fold twist; end twist (a variation of the bear ear twist); multi-twist (2 bubble); and shaping.

BALLOONS
2 differently colored 260 balloons

TWISTING TIME
With practice, you can create this design in under 30 seconds

1. Inflate the 1st balloon.

2. We'll start with the head of the snake. First we need a 1" **End Twist:** This is a variation of a fold twist, very similar but much easier than the bear ear twist you will be learning later. An end twist always has the knot of the balloon as one side of the bubble for the twist. In order to create this we will need to twist a bubble 1" down the balloon starting on the end that has the knot. Pinch the twisted part of the balloon between your thumb and pointer and middle fingers with

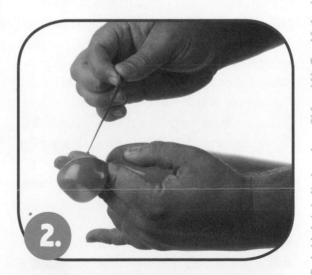

your left hand. Grab the knot of the balloon and pull it over your two fingers and around the twisted section of the balloon to where your thumb is. Push the knotted end of the balloon through the space between the twisted portion of the balloon and your pointer and middle fingers. Pull it tight and you have an end twist. We basically tied a knot with the end of the balloon around a bubble we made 1" down.

3. Next we need a 5" **Fold Twist:** Whenever we describe the length of a new twist we are describing the length of the bubble starting from the last twist we made. In this case we are measuring 5" from the End Twist, not from the end of the balloon. So we've measured up 5". Make a twist to form a new bubble. Take this new twist and fold the balloon over in the middle of the 5". Now your new twist and the previous end twist should be next to each other. Twist the end of the 5" bubble into the end twist we created earlier. Since we are twisting the balloon back into itself, the thing should hold. The end product of this twist looks much like a "U." If you have something that looks more like "II" then you put a twist in the middle when you folded and made a multi-twist. No need to feel embarrassed unless you've already proudly displayed it to all your friends.

4. Now we need a 3" **Fold Twist.** What's this? No longwinded description on how to make it? I've already explained this twist—the only difference between this one and the last is that it will be 3" rather than 5". From now on I will assume you know how to make an End Twist and Fold

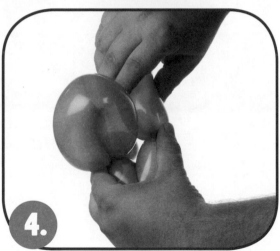

Twist. If you ever forget you can turn back here or look in the glossary in the back of the book.

5. After you finish the twist you need to align the bubbles so that the larger (5") fold twist, end twist, and the rest of the untwisted balloon are in a straight line, while the smaller (3") fold twist comes out the bottom perpendicular to the rest. This makes the larger fold twist the

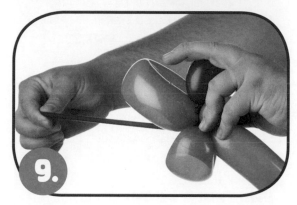

upper jaw and the smaller the lower jaw. The end bubble just helps stabilize things.

6. Our first technique, **Shaping,** is coming up. A technique is anything we do to the balloon to create new shapes that does not actually involve putting new twists into the balloon. To shape the balloon, simply take the long portion of the balloon and wrap it around two or three times until it has the look of a spring. You can hold the balloon against your body if it makes it easier. Once you have your balloon "spring," gently squeeze up and down the length of the balloon. When you let go, the snake's body should now have a nice curve to it.

7. Inflate the 2nd balloon only 3" to 4" and then tie the knot.

8. Here we are going to use our first $1\frac{1}{2}$" × $1\frac{1}{2}$" **Multi-Twist:** As mentioned before the $1\frac{1}{2}$" × $1\frac{1}{2}$" describes the length of each twist being used in the multi-twist. The base of the first twist, in this case, is at the knot. We then go up $1\frac{1}{2}$" (or half the inflated balloon) and make a twist, but we don't twist it back into the knot at this point. Instead we take the other $1\frac{1}{2}$" bubble and twist the end of it back into the knot. Since the whole inflated part of the balloon is equal to approximately 3", we don't need to actually make a second bubble— it is naturally there after the first twist. Tie the knot of the balloon around the end of the second bubble at the point where inflated goes to uninflated. Just loop it around each other once, a half a granny knot or like the first part of tying you shoes. Finally, push the lip of the balloon between the two bubbles we just made. Tie the ends of the balloon around again to ensure it stays in place, basically completing a granny knot. This will be the snake's eyes and tongue.

9. Place the eyes on top of the upper jaw where the upper jaw and the end twist meet. Hold the eyes there while you wrap the uninflated portion of the 2nd balloon around the base of the jaws in front of the end twist on the first balloon. Wrap it completely once and then pull the uninflated portion between the two fold twists (the jaws). Now we have a finished snake.

Did that seem like an awful lot of explaining just for one of the simplest balloons? It certainly was, but those are also three twists and a technique that will not need to be explained again. Almost a third of them in the first design. Just hang in there—the start is always the most daunting.

Let's review the twists and techniques we used and why.

Fold Twist: This twist is most useful when you need something round or rounded, like a person's head, flower petals, or, in this case, the jaw of a snake. If we were making a specific type of snake, like a viper, we would want something that would give a more triangular look to the head.

End Twist: This is a useful twist that often substitutes for a bear ear twist on the end of the balloon. We learn it first because it is quick and easy. We will learn the bear ear twist later.

Shaping: This is the more gradual of the

Just for Fun

As you are shaping the balloon into a spring, point it at a child who is at least a few feet back. Talk about how you like balloon snakes but you just can't trust them, they will attack without warning. Then let go of the balloon except for the end of the tail and the snake will spring at the child. Hilarity ensues. You can reassure them that it has been defanged for the child's and its own protection.

two methods in getting the balloon to curve or turn without actually twisting the balloon itself. With this you can make such things as tails, fun hats, or, in the case of this design, the snake's body.

Multi-Twist (2 bubble): Our first multi-twist. Two bubbles of the same size are used when the part of the sculpture is supposed to be symmetrical, like legs or arms, or, in this case, the snake's eyeballs. Yet sometimes it helps to make them asymmetrical, one being smaller than the other, and then the larger bubble is forced to curve. This helps in making the impression of birds' wings or beaks.

How was the snake? Don't forget to practice it. Practice is the only way you will learn to become quick and confident in the techniques we've learned. Your snake will start coming faster and looking better after only a few tries. What do you do with the multitude of snakes you've created practicing? Put them back in spring shape and hide them in drawers around the house. Or you can set them aside and learn . . .

The Twisty Sword

This design is based off of one my brother-in-law Paco created. In the years after he taught it to me, I've seen variations of it used by many balloon twisters. The twisty sword is always popular with children, if not always with parents who get whacked with it. Here are the twists and techniques you will be learning: wrap around; multi-twist (3 bubble); and break away.

BALLOONS
2 differently colored 260 balloons

TWISTING TIME
With practice, this is another 30-second design

1. We'll start by making the handle: Inflate the 1st balloon. Make a 1" end twist.

2. Make a 4" to 5" bubble: Any time we mention a bubble rather than a twist, we are referring to something that does not eventually loop back to connect into the first twist of the bubble or chain of bubbles. In this case we are making the handle of the sword, and it needs to be straight.

3. Make a 3" × 3" × 3" multi-twist: This is very similar to the 2-bubble multi-twist we learned

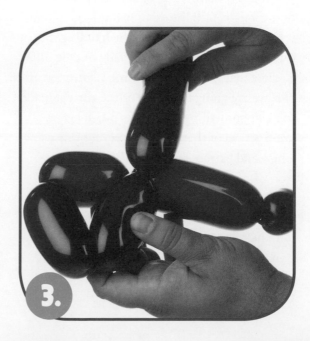

3.

earlier, with the most obvious difference being that there are three bubbles instead of two. This will be the last of the multi-twists that I explain. Just remember that format and that the start of the first bubble will be twisted into the last twist of the last bubble. In this case we will be making three bubbles before the last twist is twisted back into the first. 3" × 3" × 3" means that each bubble will be 3" long. If done correctly it should look like you have a triangle poking out of the balloon. Aren't you glad we have that done? How about we do it again?

4. Make a 3" × 3" × 3" multi-twist: Yup, the exact same thing. Just remember that the start of this multi-twist is the end of the last one you made. When you finish making this second triangle, pull the extra balloon up so that it looks vaguely sword-like, the handle going in one side and a thin straight blade out the other.

Now that we have something vaguely sword-like, we are going to get rid of the current blade to make something that looks much better. We'll get rid of that boring straight blade using a new and extremely useful technique:

5. Break Away: About 3" up from the last twist, and using your left hand, pinch the balloon between your thumb and the side of your pointer finger. With your other hand, pinch the balloon about 1½" farther up between your thumb and the side of your middle

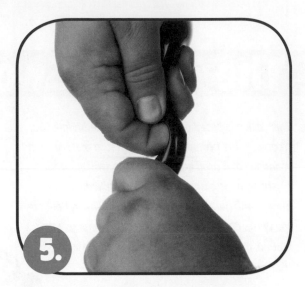

5.

finger. This should leave your pointer finger free. Use that free pointer finger to make a hook and put it against the balloon between your hands. In one motion, rock your hooked finger into the balloon while pulling the two pinched parts of the balloon apart. You need to do it quickly and with conviction or it won't work. Put more force into it than you think necessary. Just make sure no one is behind your elbows. You should now be holding two different balloon parts, and they should still be inflated (you didn't let go of the pinches, did you?). You can carefully let go of the one that doesn't contain the handle. Now that that hand is free, use it to grab the portion of still inflated balloon where the "blade" just came up out of the multi-twists. Now you can let go of the other pinched part to let the air out and tie a knot in the balloon next to the handle to prevent further deflation.

Remember that since you are breaking the balloon, any section you want to keep inflated

each other with your right hand overlapping one portion of the balloon with the other. Move your left hand down to grab the base of each new curve and repeat. Squeeze the balloon as you curve the two portions together so that as you approach the end, the two inflated ends of the sword match. (Don't be discouraged if it doesn't happen the first time. Practice is the key.) Twist the two ends together, leaving 1" bubbles at either end.

8. Place the area where the multi-twists meet on the handle of the sword right next to where the 1" bubbles are twisted on the blade, so that the 1" bubbles fill the empty space between the triangles. Take the 1" bubble that does not end with a knot, twist it around and through the junction where the multi-twists meet on handle, the point were we broke away that extra section of balloon until it comes out to its original location (again, rolling the balloon into the twist helps). Holding both the multi-twists and the 1" bubbles, next take the twisted blade of the sword through that same motion, once around and between the ends of the multi-twists. This will help strengthen the blade. (For some reason swords get a lot of abuse.) For purely cosmetic reasons you may want to twist or tie the end of the knot and any uninflated balloon into the handle where the multi-twists meet.

will need to be tied. We could have tied and saved the other portion of the balloon as well by holding it in our mouth or having someone else hold it until the handle portion was tied and then tying the straight portion. In this case we didn't need the straight portion so we let it deflate. You now have your handle (and a dead worm).

6. Inflate the 2nd balloon, leaving only 1" to 2" uninflated.

7. Wrap Around: Fold the whole balloon in half. With your left hand, hold the top of the fold. Curve each half of the balloon around

You now have a twisty sword, or, as my brother-in-law likes to call it, THE FLAMING SWORD OF JUSTICE. Yes, the capital letters were necessary.

Let's review the twists and techniques we used and why.

Wrap Around: I use this when I need a long length of balloon that is also sturdy, or a bit thicker than a single balloon width. It works well to make a bow and arrow since the sturdiness of the balloon creates some spring. Here we take advantage of the sturdiness to make the blade of the sword, which is likely to see a lot of use. I also use this in my wiener dog design—it makes the body thicker, sturdier, and more interesting than using a single width of balloon.

Multi-Twist (3 bubble): This is really a variation on the multi-twist we learned earlier, but here we are using three symmetrical bubbles instead of two. With some modification, that triangle shape can be the chest of a superhero or even the triangular head of a viper, like we discussed in the last design. Using more bubbles would result in a square, pentagon,

Have you practiced that sword a few times? Is your family beginning to complain that there is nowhere to sit because balloons are occupying every free space? Then you are on the right track. If you need to give yourself more room, just remember that the pin is mightier than the balloon sword.

Just for Fun

After completing the handle for the sword and breaking away the extra, give the handle to the child. State that it is a safety sword—it has no blade so the child can't hurt himself. Just remember to make the rest of the sword before the child starts to cry.

etc. The problem is that the more bubbles you make, the more the sculpture will want to come untwisted. Those bear ears I mentioned in the last design can help with that problem. I will teach you about them soon. I promise.

Break Away: This is one of the most useful things I learned while doing balloons. It therefore surprised me how few books actually teach how to do it. If you become proficient at it, it will cut the amount of twisting time in half while at the same time being the single most incredible thing to those who you perform for. This technique can help if you've filled a balloon up more than it needs (like we did with the sword) or if you didn't inflate it enough. If we know we don't have enough inflated balloon to finish out a design, we can break away and tie in a fresh, adequately pumped balloon without having to start from scratch.

The Daisy Flower

I've often said that if you know how to make a sword and a flower, ninety-five percent of all children will be happy. Prepare to make the world a happier place for children everywhere (or at least within fifty feet of you, and only while you are twisting balloons). Here is the technique you will be learning: push bubble.

BALLOONS
2 differently colored size 260 balloons

TWISTING TIME
Yet another design that, with practice, can be made in less than 30 seconds.

1. We'll make the stem first. Inflate the 1st balloon, leaving 3" to 4" uninflated. Make a 5" bubble, 5" fold twist, and another 5" fold twist that twists into the same area as the first to create a set of leaves. This will look similar to the sword handle we just learned, except less triangular.

2. Moving down from the other non-knotted end of the balloon, twist a 1" bubble out of the last of the inflated part of the balloon.

3. Now we move onto that new technique: Make a **Push Bubble** by pinching and pulling the uninflated end of the balloon a few times to help weaken it so the air will want to flow into it. (If you pull and let go it makes a very satisfying snapping noise). Now we just need to convince the air to move from that 1" bubble we created to the very end of the balloon while leaving the space between uninflated. With your left hand, grasp the 1" bubble you twisted so that the bubble rests on your palm and the area where the balloon transitions from inflated to uninflated is held between your thumb and the edge of your pointer finger. Held, not pinched. Air needs to be able to flow through the uninflated area but we want to keep the balloon from expanding until the very end portion. Squeeze the bottom of the bubble in your hand while keeping your thumb and pointer finger securely around the uninflated part of the balloon. A bubble should appear at the end of the balloon. Pinch right below the new bubble to keep air from going back. Squeeze this new bubble to help convince it to be permanent. This is your first experience with the push bubble. There is a more advanced way of doing it when most of the balloon is uninflated. But we'll save that for the near future.

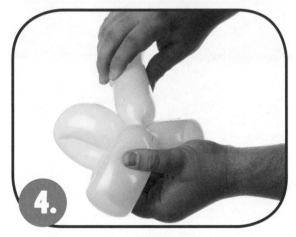

4. We still need petals for our flower. Inflate the 2nd balloon. To make the petals we'll create a series of 5" fold twists. The first 5" fold twist will be made using the knot at one end. Wrap the knot around the twist at the other end of the bubble and then push the knot through the "U" portion of the fold twist much like we did with the snake eyes. Try to push the lip of the

balloon through near the twist itself. Continue making fold twists until you run out of balloon. You'll probably end up with 5 or 6. Break away any extra.

5. Place the bubble of the 1st balloon on the center of all the fold twists in the petals. Pull the uninflated portion of the balloon through

5.

Just for Fun

Let the child know not to let the balloon hit the ground outside. We don't want the flower to change from a daisy to a "poppy!"

to the center of the petals so it comes out the other end.

You now have a flower of the daisy persuasion. Let's review what we learned and why.

Push Bubble: This twist helps give motion to your balloon creations. I use it for antennae for butterflies, slugs, or any bug. Here, we use it for the flower. I'll use it anytime I want a little animation or when something needs a ball on the end of a thin piece. Perhaps it could even be used to make a tetherball.

The Jester Hat

Hats are almost as popular as swords when it comes to balloon designs. As such, it is good to know a few basic ways to measure heads and make hats. Here is the technique you will be learning: pinch shaping.

BALLOONS
3 differently colored 260 balloons

TWISTING TIME
Yet another dazzling 30-second design (depending on how well they cooperate with the measuring part)

While I am only teaching how to make one hat here, it is a good idea for you to know a few different ways to start. That way when you start creating your own hats they don't all look the same. The principal is similar with all of them. Get one or more balloons to create a shape that can fit around someone's head. Most of the time this means you will need to measure that person's head. The easiest method is to make an end twist on an inflated balloon, and then put the balloon around the

person's head, measuring where the other end of the balloon meets the end twist. In other words, this is a glorified loop. Don't twist yet—that could get uncomfortable for the recipient. Remove the balloon from the person's head and give yourself just a little more balloon than you measured before twisting the two

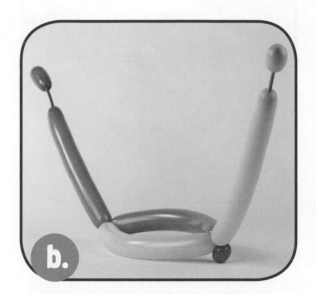

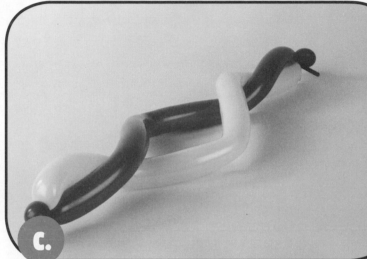

measured parts of the balloon together (**see a and b**). This basic idea can be done with as many balloons as you wish to use. You don't need to stick with just one. I find, though, that if I use more than three balloons (creating a triangle), it gets hard to do the measuring part. Just as a quick safety tip: don't make anything that will cover someone's eyes or ears. The balloons can be painful if they pop in those sensitive areas.

If you don't want to bother with measuring, here is another technique for a hat. Remember the twisty part of the sword we learned? This time, take two balloons (inflated until only 1" remains) and twist the two knotted ends together, creating 1" bubbles on the end. You can first create two end twists and then twist them together if you wish or you may put the two balloons, untwisted, next to each

other so that the knots match up then measure up about an inch and twist both balloons together as if you were putting a twist in a single balloon. Now do that whole wrap around technique until you can twist 1" bubbles on the other end. If you pull at the wrap-around part, it will open up enough to put on a head (**see c**). The bigger the head, the more you pull. (Just be sensitive when you make comments about their head size.)

Here are the instructions for making the Jester Hat, pictured on the opposite page.

1. Inflate the 1st balloon. Make a 1" end twist.

2. Inflate the 2nd balloon. Make a 1" end twist.

3. Inflate the 3rd balloon. Make a 1" end twist.

4. Here comes the tricky part. You've got to measure the person's head, trying to get it so that each of the three balloons evenly and equally encompasses the head. The way to do this is to hold all three balloons so that they form a triangle with three equal sides. One balloon will overlap another at each of the end twists—don't try to use the whole balloon to make the triangle. Put this triangle up to the person's head and adjust the triangle to make it smaller or bigger as needed before you twist. Make sure to keep the sides all of equal length. Once you have the right size, make it a tiny bit larger, because the bubbles have a tendency to get smaller as you twist them. Since all three sides are going to be equal, you only need to keep holding two of the balloons at this point. Pick two and hold them where the end twist of one balloon crosses the other balloon. Twist them together by pinching that point on the balloon and twisting the end twist around it.

5. Measure up the connected balloons from end twist to end twist to find out how long it was. Each side of the triangle will need to be that long. Measure that length from the end twist that is currently attached to the other balloon (you should be measuring the balloon that is the same color as the end twist we mentioned). You should still have one unattached balloon. Place the currently unattached balloon's end twist at the point measured on

the last balloon and twist it in as we did before. You now have all three balloons attached to each other, but you need to make them into a triangle. One of the balloon ends will seem longer than the others—this is the one to twist into the last available end twist. The length needs to be the same as the others. You now have a triangle with three lengths of balloon poking out from the corners. Grab each of the three lengths and pull them to the center. Give each enough length so that when the original triangle is placed over the person's head, the top of the hat doesn't stop it from going on (about 7" or so). Twist the three together. Now you have a pyramid with balloon lengths poking out from the top. Next we use what is called pinch shaping.

6. Pinch Shaping: Again, this is a technique—we are not making any twists in the balloon, merely shaping it. Two or three times on each balloon, fold that balloon over and, between your thumb and the length of your

6.

7. At the end of each balloon, make a 1" push bubble. If there is no uninflated end on the balloon, don't worry about it—just don't make a push bubble.

One jester hat ready to be worn. Tell the recipient he has to supply his own jokes.

Let's review what we learned and why:

Pinch Shaping: This is the other shaping method, the less gradual one, mentioned when we made the snake. I use this when I want sharp but graceful turns in a balloon design, like for a princess's arm, a monkey's tail, or, in this case, extra flair for the jester hat.

pointer finger, pinch the outside half of the fold. Twist the pinched area slightly as you let go. The pinched area should now have a 45- to 90-degree bend depending on how hard you pinched and how much you twisted. As was mentioned, do this two or three times on each length of balloon.

You've learned some decent designs by this time. Your ability to twist has most likely come a long way. This next design will teach you perhaps the most-used twist in small designs: the bear ear. It is not a particularly hard twist, but it looks like it should be, and so it intimidates a lot of people. However, intimidating as it looks, it is vital that you learn it; most designs use it somehow . . . you've just been lucky up until now.

The Butterfly

You have twenty flowers lying around, right? Such a garden deserves a few butterflies. Here are the twists and techniques you will be learning: twist of thirds (it doesn't really have a name, so I made one up); bear ear twist (commonly referred to simply as bear ear, or double bear ears if two are next to each other); and advanced push bubble.

BALLOONS
3 differently colored 260 balloons

TWISTING TIME
Another 30–40 second-er

1. First we need some wings. Inflate the 1st balloon until only 1" to 2" remain uninflated on the end.

2. Let's do that **Twist of Thirds:** About a third of the way in from each end of the balloon, fold the balloon so that the end of each side of the balloon finishes at the fold at the opposite side. In the middle of this folded excitement, twist the three balloon segments together.

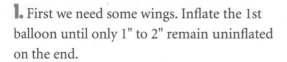

3.

4.

Bear Ear: This is just a very small fold twist. In order to make it, first create a 1" bubble and fold either side of the bubble so that they may be held in one hand. This means that first 1" bubble that contains the knot, and the long portion of the balloon after the 2nd 1" bubble should fit in your hand leaving that 2nd 1" bubble visible and accessible. This should leave one hand free and the 1" bubble accessible. We are going to twist the two ends of the 2nd 1" bubble together, but you may have noticed it seems a little tight. The easiest way to twist the two ends of the bubble closer together is to pull out on the center of the 1" bubble as you twist it. As you pull out, it brings the two ends together and makes your job a lot easier. Got it? Good—you'll have plenty of chances to practice!

5. Make another 1" bear ear. Adjust the 1" bubble so that it comes out one side of the pair of bear ears and the rest of the balloon comes out the other end in a straight line. Make a 1½" bubble and a 1" bear ear.

6. Twist the latest bear ear twist into the middle of the first balloon—the center of the wings. Wrap the long part of the balloon once around the twist at the center of the wings so that the portion of the balloon that has the

3. You should have two loops and two much shorter ends of the balloon. Tie each end of the balloon back into the middle twist, making two more smaller fold twists. This should make two large wings and two small ones for your butterfly.

4. Let's make the body of the butterfly. Inflate the 2nd balloon. Make a 1" bubble. Make a 1"

double bear ears comes out from between the two large wings, and the long part of the balloon comes out from between the smaller pair of wings.

7. Make a 1½" bubble, and then break away and tie the balloon.

8. Advanced Push Bubble: We need some butterfly antennae. Inflate only 3" of the 3rd balloon. Make a 1½" bubble. Now you are going to do another push bubble, like you did for the Daisy Flower (page 25). The concept is the same, but the execution is a little more complicated. First, pinch and pull the end of the balloon like you did last time. You still need the bubble that is going to be pushed in the palm of your hand so that you can squeeze it. We still need to squeeze it from one end to the other. The difference is the distance. We have a lot more balloon that we need to keep uninflated, so we have to figure out a new way to hold it to keep those parts from inflating. Form the bubble to be pushed and hold it in your left palm. About a half an inch up from where the balloon becomes uninflated, fold it over and run the uninflated part of the balloon back down along your fingers in the same hand. Fold the balloon again and run it back up the same way, putting your other hand over the whole thing and leaving just the end of the balloon visible and able to expand.

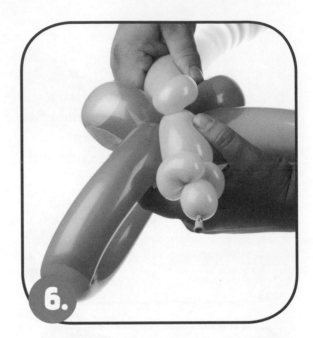

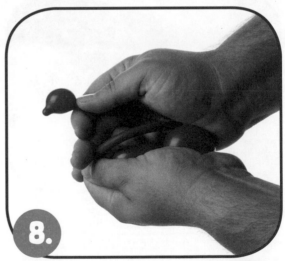

Now squeeze that bubble while keeping all but the other end of the balloon uninflated. You may close your hands over the whole thing. The picture shows the hands open so you may see how the balloon is positioned.

9. Pinch the middle of the balloon, then place the pinched part on the 2nd balloon where the bear ears meet. While pinching, wrap the balloon in the center around the bear ears so that both antennae come out from the top.

Now you have your butterfly. Let's review what you have learned and why:

Twist of Thirds: This is a unique use of the fold twists. In fact, the only thing that makes this worth calling attention to is that it allows you to quickly and fairly accurately divide the balloon into thirds. By folding it over other ways you can get quarters or fifths and so on.

Bear Ear Twist: We finally learned it. This is the most common twist used in all of balloondom. It is a stabilizing force and allows for the balloon to change direction. If we use just one bear ear, then the balloon changes direction about 90 degrees. If we use two bear ears together, they can be used like a hinge and we can have the angle be anything we

choose—though, unless otherwise stated, most of the designs in the book will have the balloon go straight into and out of a pair of bear ears (or double bear ears, as I like to call them) without any angle change at all. This is in part because bear ears are used as often as connection points for other balloons, or as stabilizing points on a balloon, as they are to actually create certain shapes. I certainly use them for specific shapes though. I use the bear ear for elbows on people, animal nostrils, and eyeballs, to name a few. The twist gets easier the more you practice and, again, we will give you plenty of chances for that practice.

The Monkey with a Banana

At this point, you've learned almost every twist that this book teaches. I still have a few more techniques that I personally find useful before we get into the meat of how to design your own sculptures. This little monkey is quick and quite popular. He'll have them calling (or howling) for more. Here is the technique you will be learning: squeeze and pull.

BALLOONS
1 brown size 260 balloon
1 yellow size 260 balloon

TWISTING TIME
30–40 seconds

1. Let's make a banana: Inflate the 1st balloon (yellow). Make a 3" bubble. Break away the rest. Feel free to shape a little curve into the banana, if you wish. Repeat for up to three bananas from the same balloon if you'll be making a lot of monkeys.

2. Now let's make a monkey head: Inflate the 2nd balloon (brown). Make a 2" bubble, 1" bear ear, 2" bubble, and 1" bear ear. Twist the end knot into the second bear ear. Make a 2½" bubble twisted into the first bear ear (this will

be the front of the face).

3. This is a great monkey head—except for the fact that the neck comes out of one of the ears. I find that distracting. So we'll see if we can get it to come out of the head instead.

To do that we'll need a new technique: **Squeeze and Pull.** At the place where the rest of the balloon comes out from the bear ear, squeeze the balloon to push some of the air down. While holding that squeezed part, pull the squeezed part of the balloon between

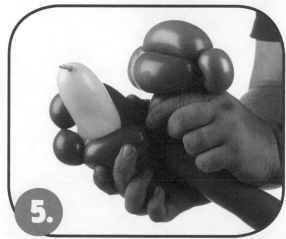

Just for Fun

Hand over the banana before you make the monkey. Once the child is holding the banana say, "Look, a monkey holding a banana!"

banana between all the bubbles and then twist the multi-twist into place. Remember that if you hold onto the first twist in a series and the last twist, it will keep all the ones between from coming undone. This can be a little tricky at first, but if you learn to hold the balloon against your body to stabilize it and learn how to hold the whole thing in one hand when putting the banana in, then it becomes much, much easier. Make a 1½" bubble.

6. For the legs, make a 1½" x 1½" multi-twist. Add two pinch shapings to help shape the tail, if it isn't too tight.

Let's review what we learned and why.

Squeeze and Pull: This is a graceful solution to get the balloon to exit a group of bubbles from the middle rather than either edge. It can be used for dragonfly heads or hands on more complicated designs, and it is excellent for monkey heads. You may notice as you start practicing the monkey that the neck tends to slip back to the ear. As you finish the design, just repeat the Squeeze and Pull. As you get more experienced with how to hold the balloons comfortably, this problem should happen less and less.

the front of the bubble that makes the face and either of the other two 2" bubbles. As we let the squeezed part go, the balloon reinflates and holds the neck in place.

4. You now have the monkey's head, but we need a neck. Make a 1½" bubble.

5. Lets make the arms around the banana. Make a 2" × 1" × 1" × 2" multi-twist, but before you finish the multi-twist, place the

The Dog

You might be wondering why the dog design is this far into the book. I mean, everyone and his dog knows how to make a balloon dog. Well, this is not your common breed of dog balloon.

Many times the twist you choose to use on a design is not the one that will make it look the best. It is the twist that will help it look the best in the amount of time you have to twist it. Here we will learn the pop twist, which is another way to make two balloons out of one. The break away can also be used, but many times the pop twist is actually faster, and it doesn't take anything away from your design.

BALLOONS
2 of the same color
and 1 differently colored size 260 balloons

TWISTING TIME
1½ minutes at advanced twisting speed

1. Inflate the 1st balloon (same color as second balloon), leaving 2" to 3" uninflated at the end.

2. Here we will be creating the head and one of the legs. Make a 2" bubble and 2" × 2" multi-twist. Tie the knot of the balloon into the middle twist of the 2-bubble multi-twist to create three bubbles together. This will be the

dog's snout. Make a 1" bear ear, 1½" bubble, 1" bear ear (we will twist the ears in here later), and 1½" bubble twisted back into the first bear ear. This is basically the head. Later we will add ears and a nose.

3. Now let's make a neck: Make a 1½" bubble, 1" bear ear, and 1" bear ear. The double bear

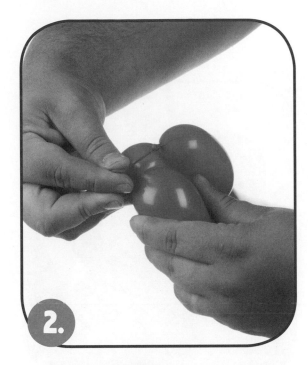

2.

4.

4. Now onto the first leg: Make a 2" bubble, 1" bear ear, and 2½" to 3" fold twist. Break away the rest if there is extra. We now have a one-legged puppy dog with no ears or nose. You probably don't want to hand it out like that.

5. Let's make the other front leg: Inflate the 2nd balloon (same color as 1st balloon). Make a 1" end twist, 2½" to 3" fold twist, and 2" bubble twisted into the double bear ears on the last balloon to create a second leg. Adjust so that the end of the balloon comes out perpendicular to the front legs and come out the opposite direction than the head faces.

6. Now onto the body: Make a 3" bubble and 1" bear ear.

7. Rear legs would be nice too. Make a 2" bubble. Here we will make our **Pop Twist:** Since we are going to pop the balloon like in the break away technique, we need to do something to keep it from deflating. In this case we can't really tie a knot, so we twist, and twist, and twist until the balloon is so twisted the air just can't get through. Any twist—bear ear, fold, or multi-twist—that may be next to the bubble we are going to pop needs to be twisted about 7 times. Let's go ahead and do that: Make a 1" bear ear (twisted 7 times), 2½" to 3" fold twist

ears will allow us to tie the other front leg and the body onto what we are now creating. The neck should come into one side of the bear ears and the rest of the balloon come out the opposite side.

(twisted 7 times), 1" bubble, 1" bear ear (twisted 7 times), 2½" to 3" fold twist (twisted 7 times), and 2" bubble twisted back into where the body and rear legs connect. The rest of the balloon makes a tail coming out the back.

8. Now back to the pop twist. You created a 1" bubble between the two back legs (the one between all the "twisted 7 times" remarks). We are going to pop that bubble. I use my finger-nails between my thumb and pointer finger to grab a small portion of the balloon and then quickly pull to pop it. Sometimes it takes a couple of tries for the better quality balloons. I have a friend who prefers to pull out his keys or some pointy object to pop the bubble. Feel free to try either way.

9. Here we will make the nose and ears: Inflate the 3rd balloon (the different color) to 6". Twist a 1" bubble and break away, keeping both sections inflated. This should leave you with a 1" bubble to make a nose and separately a 4" to 5" bubble with a length of uninflated balloon for the ears. Hold one of the inflated fragments in your mouth to keep it from deflating while you tie the other one. Don't put it inside your mouth! Hold the end of it with your lips— none of the balloon should actually be inside your mouth. (If you have some aversion to putting a balloon up to your lips, have a friend hold it for you).

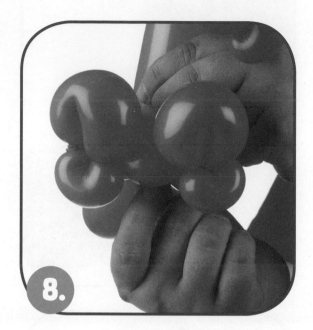

10. Once both are tied, take the 1" bubble and tie both ends of it into the end of the 3-bubble structure we built on the first balloon. This is the dog's nose.

11. Take the other portion of balloon and twist halfway up the 4" to 5" bubble and then create a push bubble the same way we did with the butterfly. Twist the center of the balloon into the lone bear ear on the top of the head to form some floppy ears.

You now have a dog. Don't worry—they come housebroken. Let's review what we learned and why.

Pop Twist: This is another time- and

11.

balloon-saving technique. Conceivably you could use a break away any time you wanted to do this, but that actually uses more of your balloon in order to tie knots on either side. This, incidentally, is why we twisted each bubble 7 times. It is not quite as good as a knot, but it only comes undone on rare occasions and with really determined children.

Just for Fun

Before you hand the finished dog over, tell the child that the dog knows tricks. Hold the dog up and tell it to "play dead," then let the dog fall over. Just make sure to catch it before it hits the ground.

The Jet Plane

It is good to have some sort of motorized vehicle in your repertoire. Motorcycles, tractors, planes, and trains are the most popular. This jet plane offers a new technique called balloon stuffing. This is where you place something inside the balloon itself. In this case we are simply making a bubble and pushing it inside the balloon. It is a fun method to use once you get it down, and it is always a crowd pleaser—at least for the small crowd that can see what you are doing. This project will teach you the balloon stuffing technique.

BALLOONS
1 gray 260 balloon
1 clear 260 balloon
2 black 260 balloons

TWISTING TIME
2 minutes

1. We will start with the body of the jet. Inflate the 1st balloon (gray). Make a 1" bubble, 1" bear ear, and 1" bear ear. Make the balloon come straight out through the double bear ears. Make a 2" bubble, 1" bear ear, and 1" bear ear. Again, the balloon should come straight out through the bear ears. Make a 2½" bubble, 1" bear ear, 1" bear ear, and 2½" bubble twisted back into the second pair of bear ears we made.

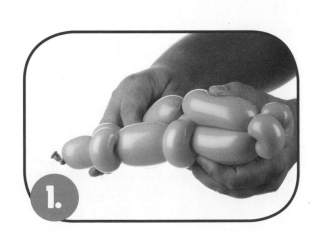

The rear of the jet is the other end with the two bear ears.

3. We need the wings and the jet tail. These will be mirror images of each other, so it is easiest if we go ahead and make both and then slightly adjust one to create the mirror image. First, the tail: Inflate the 2nd balloon (black). Make a 1" end twist and 1" × 1" × 1" multi-twist.

4. Now the wing: Continue with the same balloon. Make a 2½" bubble, 1" bear ear, 3" bubble, 1" bubble, and 2½" bubble twisted into the end twist, and then break away, again leaving as much uninflated balloon left as possible. Repeat steps 3 and 4 with the 3rd balloon (black) to make the other section of the tail and wing.

5. You have made the wings and tail (the tail being the multi-twist). Choose one of the wings and twist the tail section to the other side so that the two wings are mirror images of each other.

6. Place both wings, one on either side, next to the pair of 2½" bubbles on the first balloons. The tail (multi-twists) should be near the rear section of the jet. The only other bear ears on the wings should be near that long, uniflated

2. Now we are going to break away, but we want a good long portion of uninflated balloon when we are done. So break away farther out than you need to, yet tie the knot close to the bear ears. Fight the urge to twist all that extra uninflated balloon into the bear ears—we'll need it later. The front of the jet will be where the original knot was made.

portion of balloon we left on the jet body. That long piece of uninflated gray balloon should wrap around the bear ear of each wing and between the double bear ears on the gray. This is easiest done if the gray bear ears are vertical so that the black bear ears in the wing have a place to nuzzle against. The uninflated balloon portions on each of the wings near the tail should each be wrapped into the bear ears on the back of the plane.

7. Now for the cockpit. Inflate the 4th balloon (clear). Make a ½" bubble.

8. Balloon Stuffing: The important thing about this bubble is that it be smaller than the diameter of the rest of the balloon. We are going to be pushing this small bubble into the balloon (**see 8a**). With your pointer finger, push that bubble into the rest of the balloon, using your other fingers to stabilize the bubble as you push it (**see 8b**). Once the bubble is inside the balloon, hold onto it with your free hand and carefully pull your pointer finger out just a little bit. Then form a hook and pull like you do with the break away technique (**see 8c**). Since the balloon has overlapped itself, you should have a bubble roaming free inside the balloon. Pinch the top of the balloon as you remove your inserted finger and then tie it off with the knot we learned at the beginning of the book. You can treat it as if you were tying

Now you can sing a John Denver song and hand the balloon over. Let's review what we learned and why.

Balloon Stuffing: Besides being cool to look at, this technique has a lot of applications. I use it for a lot of sports-themed balloons when I want the ball to move. You can use it for joeys in kangaroos, peas in a pod, even googlie eyes.

a newly inflated balloon. Just make sure the bubble is free before you tie the balloon off.

9. Make a 2" bubble (with inserted bubble inside it) and break away (tying the other end of the 2" bubble after you have broken it off). Tie one end onto where the first set of double bear ears are on the 1st balloon. Tie the other end where the second set of double bear ears are on the 1st balloon (where the wings first enter in) to form a cockpit with a pilot.

The Princess

This design is the only time I touch on any kind of weaving in this book. Weaving is generally reserved for making large sculptures that can literally use hundreds of balloons. It is a technique with enough material for a book in its own right. The simple weaving pattern presented here, however, works well on a small scale for a number of graceful designs—one of which, my favorite, is the princess. You will learn these twists and techniques: rose weave and tulip twist.

BALLOONS

4 light blue 260 balloons
1 blush or light brown
(basically a skin color) 260 balloon
1 yellow or dark brown
(a hair color of your choice) 260 balloon
1 red 160 balloon (remember, if you don't
have 160s yet, don't panic—just replace the 160
with a 260 any time that comes along)

TWISTING TIME

2 to 3 minutes with a bit of practice

1. We'll start by making the lower part of the dress. **Rose Weave:** Inflate the 1st, 2nd, and 3rd balloons (light blue) so that 1" or less remains uninflated at the end.

Tie each into a loop, with the knotted end tied to the uninflated portion of the same balloon. You should have three separate loops.

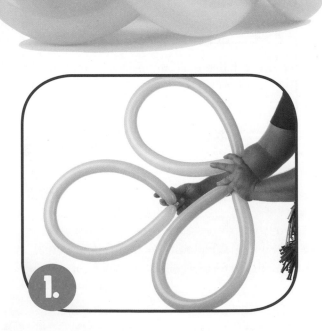

2a.

2b.

2. Place the loops side by side so that you can hold all three loops where the knot and uninflated ends meet. Your other hand can hold all

3a.

three about halfway around the loops (**see 2a**).

Twist all three together by pushing your hands together and twisting (**see 2b**). You should have six fairly equal loops that resemble flower petals.

3. Choose two "petals" of the flower that are next to each other. Make it so that the petal on the right side overlaps the one on the left. Keep your thumb on the portion of that petal that overlaps and wrap the rest of the fingers of that hand around the portion of the other petal being overlapped. If you keep your hand near the center, where the loops connect, it will make the whole process easier. Push down with your thumb and pull up with your fingers until the two portions have switched places. If you have small hands like my wife, you may need to use both hands to do it (**see 3a**). The petal that had originally overlapped is now primed to be overlapped itself. Take the next petal to the right and have it overlap the free edge of that petal. Repeat the process until you have done it to each petal. Keep using the same thumb to push down—it makes it easier to remember which balloon to push and which to pull. You have successfully woven the dress, though it may look a little flat right now (**see 3b**). If it is flat, you may want to push down along the circumference of the weave at this point to make it even more dome and dress-like (**see 3c**).

4. We have the bottom of the dress, so let's go ahead and make the top, starting with one side. Inflate the 4th balloon (light blue). Make a 2" bubble.

5. And then a poofy sleeve: Make a 1" bear ear, 1" bear ear, and 2½" fold twist.

6. The very top of the dress: Make a 1" bubble, 1" bear ear (where the head will connect), and 1" bubble.

7. The other poofy sleeve: Make a 1" bear ear, 1" bear ear, and 2½" fold twist.

8. The other side of the top portion of the dress: Make a 2" bubble twisted into the three (1st, 2nd, and 3rd) balloons where they all meet. Also tie the knot of the 4th balloon into

8.

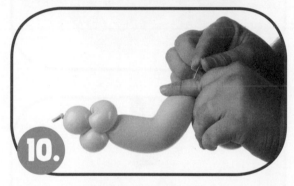

10.

11.

Inflate the 5th balloon (skin color). Make a 1" bubble, 1" bear ear, and 1" bear ear.

10. Now the arm and elbow: Make a 2" bubble and use a pinch shaping 1" up, then break away, saving the rest of the balloon. Remember to tie both ends. Repeat once more for the other arm, again saving the last bit of balloon for the head. After tying off the portion for the head, it helps to pull at the knot while gently squeezing the other end of the balloon to create a small uninflated portion at the end you were squeezing.

11. Tie each of the arms (and not the hand side of the arm) separately into each of the fold twists on the 4th balloon (one arm on each side, please). Do it on the side farthest from the bear ears and closest to the dome of the dress.

the same area. Make a 2½" bubble twisted into the single bear ear of the 4th balloon and break away. It should look dress-like, with the poofy sleeves off to either side and the dome of the dress underneath. Some people find it easier to put the top of the dress on the bottom before it is woven. For instructional purposes I didn't want the top of the dress to get in the way while we taught the weaving. Don't feel afraid to change these designs and make them your own.

9. Let's make an arm, starting with the hand.

That way the arms come out the poofy sleeves.

12. Tie the head (using the uninflated portion) into the single bear ear on the 4th balloon.

13. Time for some hair: Inflate the 6th balloon (the hair-colored one). Make a 1" bubble and 1" bear ear. Tie the other end of the head (5th balloon) to the bear ear we just made. Make a bubble the length of the head and twist the end into the section where the head and dress meet. Make a 3" fold twist. Make another bubble that goes the length of the head up into our bear ear. Make one last bubble that goes the length of the head down to where we made our fold twist and twist it in. Then break away.

14. We'll go ahead and do one more thing, teach one last twist. How about we make a flower for her hand? Inflate the 7th balloon (red) only about ½". **Tulip Twist:** This is similar to the balloon stuffing we did in the Jet (page 44), only we aren't putting a bubble inside and we aren't breaking anything away. Put your finger on the knot of the balloon and push that knot inside the balloon until it touches the uninflated end (**see 14a**). Grab the knot with your free hand through the uninflated balloon, carefully remove your finger from inside of the balloon, and twist the bubble a few times. Then, while keeping the

14b.

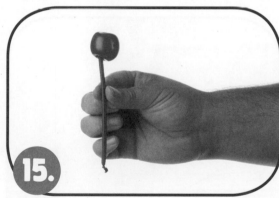

15.

After the dress is complete but before you add the
arms or head, place the dress on your own head.
Let the audience know that the dress is just a little
too small to get over your head.

Just for Fun

After the dress is complete but before you add the
arms or head, place the dress on your own head.
Let the audience know that the dress is just a little
too small to get over your head.

stem, tie a knot. Get rid of the rest of the stem.
The break away technique does not work well
with uninflated balloons, so use a small pair
of scissors or a letter opener to cut at the point
after the knot we just made.

16. Twist the stem about 1" down from the
tulip twist into the double bear ears that make
up one of the princess' hands.

She is finished! Change the colors of the
dress and the hair, figure out a few different
hairstyles, and you can make many different
princesses with this design.

You should be proud of yourself. From now
on the designs don't get harder. A few are as
difficult, but none are harder.

Let's review what we have learned and why.

Rose Weave: This particular type of weaving was taught to me as a way to create a large
flower. I have never heard a name for it, so I
call it the rose weave. Since then it has become
a princess dress and a fancy parasol. This is
only one of four or five basic types of weaving.

spot twisted, squeeze the bubble a little bit. It
will most likely stay twisted though this one
can get temperamental. Hopefully you can get
it to stay before you too get temperamental
(**see 14b**).

15. Now we have a little flower with a very
long stem. About 2"–4" down this uninflated

The other styles lend themselves more to large (over 2' designs) and I use them regularly to create custom shapes.

Tulip Twist: This creates a unique shape that has potential for many things. I use it to create small top hats, the center of a propeller on a plane, or headlights on a motorcycle. You can also do this twist when the balloon is fully inflated. The process is generally the same. Push the knot into the inflated balloon about 1" to 1½". You can feel through the inflated portion of the balloon the knot you tied at the end of the balloon. Make a twist in the balloon just above this knot and before your finger. Don't twist your finger. Gently remove your finger and the tulip twist should remain. If you want to make a tulip twist that is a little sturdier, then create a small ½" bubble at the knotted end of the balloon. It is important that this bubble be smaller than the diameter of the balloon, just like when we do balloon stuffing.

Push that bubble into the balloon about 1" to 1½". Now twist the outer inflated balloon into the twist that is between your finger and that ½" bubble and is in the interior of the balloon. Remove your finger gently.

You've made it. After this, you have all the basic techniques and twists you need for creating designs. The jet and the princess are two of the hardest designs in the book and they teach some advanced concepts. (That's my way of saying you are doing really well.) Most likely you can even look at other people's designs and figure them out. You've done well. Next we'll talk about some of the tools that might help you create a new design completely from scratch.

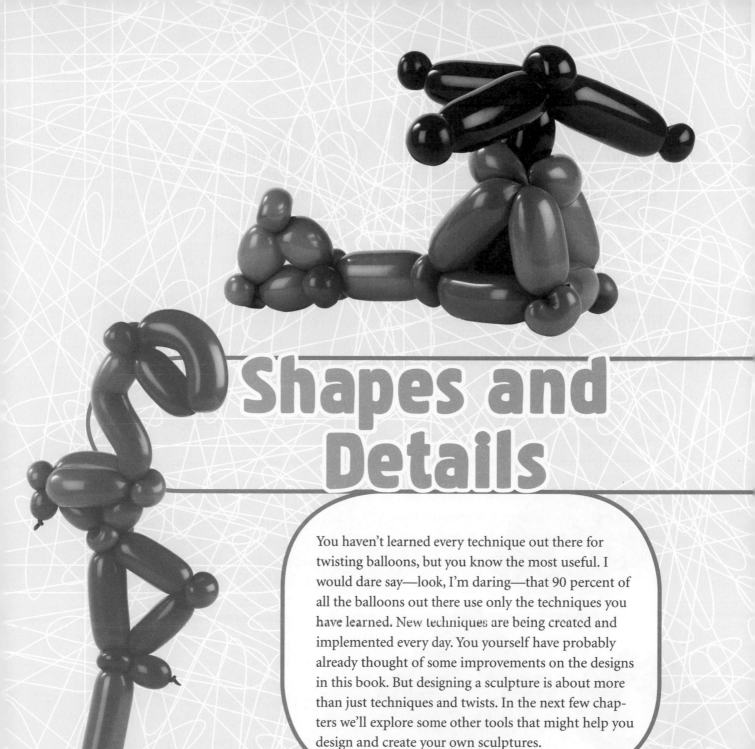

Shapes and Details

You haven't learned every technique out there for twisting balloons, but you know the most useful. I would dare say—look, I'm daring—that 90 percent of all the balloons out there use only the techniques you have learned. New techniques are being created and implemented every day. You yourself have probably already thought of some improvements on the designs in this book. But designing a sculpture is about more than just techniques and twists. In the next few chapters we'll explore some other tools that might help you design and create your own sculptures.

Shape Up, Down, and Sideways

This is an important skill for any type of art. It is also one of the most basic, and it is quite possible you already do it without thinking. If you already intuitively break down subjects for a new design into basic shapes, good for you. If you have no idea what I'm talking about, then it is time to "shape up." (If you need to take a break after that horrible pun, I understand. Just come back soon.)

Most things can be broken down into simple shapes, or a combination of simple shapes. A cardboard box is a cube, a basketball is a sphere, the Pyramids are . . . pyramid. Even complex objects are a series of shapes put together. Your hand is a series of five cylinders attached to a pentagon.

How detailed you make the sculpture—meaning how many shapes you break the object into—is one of the determining factors on how accurate your finished sculpture looks. Here's the catch. At this size we have very little detail we can work with. This being the case, we have to pick out the most basic shapes that carry the impression of what we are trying to design. In short, my friends, we are impressionists. But hopefully you won't have to die before people realize your artistic worth.

How do we decide what shapes are most important? In the end the style you personally develop will help you determine how much detail to use. The other deciding factor is how much time you have to create the sculpture. Time restraints influence this art more than any other thing. The detail you can add at a county fair with hundreds of kids lined up is very different than at a birthday party where there are ten or twelve children.

If you are having trouble figuring out what

shapes are important to put into the design, try these tips.

Do you tend to overcomplicate? Do you add so much detail that in the end it just looks like clutter rather than the object you were trying to sculpt? If so try this: Look briefly at the object you are trying to design and then look away. Then on a piece of paper draw out the basic shapes you remember in the object. At a glance your mind should record the important shapes that give the feel of the object. Now try to design the sculpture just with those shapes. Afterward you may fill in any details that seem to be missing but are necessary. Just remember to do it in context of the amount of time you have to twist the finished design.

Or . . .

Do you oversimplify? If someone were to ask you to build a snake, would you hand over an inflated, untwisted balloon? In some ways you've got it easier than our friend above who likes to overcomplicate. If you feel your designs are too simple to be recognizable, ask yourself what parts you feel are missing. In the case of the snake, an inflated, untwisted balloon gives no clue as to where the head might be. A few twists later and suddenly the design doesn't

feel so awkward. In your case, I suggest you design and make a sculpture, and then step back and look at it. What about the actual object (in terms of shapes) makes it look like the object? Add a thing or two and step back again. Does it look better or worse?

With either of these approaches, take the finished design to a friend and have him or her tell you what they think it is. If they can tell what it is without you telling them, odds are you've captured the essence of the object.

This an example of a design taken too far. I wanted to create a starfish design that people would know was a starfish and not just a star. So I figured out the star first and then started adding details. You can see the result for yourself.

The Starfish

1. First we will make a pentagon for the center of the body. This means each bubble coming out a double bear ear will be slightly angled. Inflate the 1st balloon (color 1), leaving perhaps 4" uninflated at the end. Make a 1" end twist, 1" bear ear, 2" bubble, 1" bear ear, 1" bear ear, 2" bubble, 1" bear ear, 1" bear ear, 2" bubble, 1" bear ear, 1" bear ear, 2" bubble, 1" bear ear, 1" bear ear, and 2" bubble twisted back into the first end twist/bear ear set and break away. You should now have that pentagon with a lot of bear ears. (If not, you should be able to adjust it so it becomes a pentagon with a lot of bear ears.)

2. Let's make the points on the star. Inflate the 2nd balloon (color 2). Tie the end of this balloon into the end twist/bear ear set on the first balloon. Make a 2" bubble, 2" bubble twisted into the next double bear ear on the left (**see 2a**), 2" bubble, 2" bubble twisted into the next double bear ear on the left, 2" bubble, 2" bubble twisted into the next double bear ear on the left, 2" bubble, 2" bubble twisted into the next

double bear ear on the left, 2" bubble, and 2" bubble twisted into the next and original end twist/bear ear set.

2b.

You should now have what looks like a star **(see 2b).** This would be good for most occasions when asked for a starfish. But I thought, what if you wanted to make sure no one could mistake it for just a star? What about the tube feet on the bottom of the starfish? Maybe take a white balloon and create a series of small bubbles on each of the legs to indicate those tube feet? Most starfish also have a little dot on their back. We could do a tulip twist in a balloon and attach it, off center, to the middle of the star.

Looking at both the designs together, the simpler design is still better. Sure, the other starfish has more detail, but the detail doesn't make it end up looking more like a starfish—in fact, the detail actually makes it confusing. This is the point where you would decide to try something new or stick with the simpler

design. In my case I think the simple star works fine as the shape or the animal.

So what did we learn? Detail is only important insomuch as it helps people understand the design. Sometimes too much detail can actually hinder your attempts.

The Pink Flamingo

Here is another example that shows it is not the number of details but which details you add that make for a good design. Think about a pink flamingo. What makes it a flamingo? The beak is one main feature—the top of the beak is much bigger than the bottom. The neck is long and skinny, often in an "S" shape. The body is relatively small, with the tail turned down. The legs are long and skinny and flamingoes often stand with one leg up.

BALLOONS
1 hot pink 260 balloon
2 orange 260 balloons

TWISTING TIME
About 40 seconds

1. Let's do a couple of small bubbles for the eyes and at the same time create a place where we can add the beak later.

2. Inflate the 1st balloon (pink). Make a 1" end twist, 1" bear ear, and 3" to 4" shaping into an "S" shape (for that skinny neck).

3. Now we need that small body. Make a 1" bear ear twist, 3" bubble, 1" bear ear (this is the rear of the body where the tail will come out), 3" bubble twisting it back into the first bear ear where the neck is, and 2" bubble.

2.

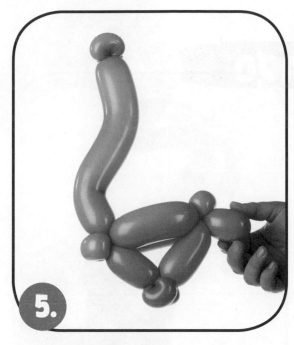

5. Now the tail: Connect the end of this latest 2" bubble to the single bear ear opposite the "S" neck on the balloon. Have it come out facing down opposite the direction of the neck. If the tail part of the balloon is much longer than 1" to 1½", break away the end of the balloon. Now we have the basic body shape with the tail pointed down and the neck in an "S" shape. If not, adjust it so you do. It should look a little bit like a funky ladle.

6. Now let's add that beak: Inflate the 2nd balloon (orange). Make a 5" × 3" multi-twist. Break away the excess balloon and tie together the two knotted ends. Twist the knotted end of the beak into the pink balloon between the end twist and bear ear that we started with on the 1st balloon. It's at the top of the neck. It should be tied in perpendicular to the neck so the beak points first forward and then curves down, with the 5" bubble being on top.

7. Now we are going to add those skinny legs. Inflate the 3rd balloon (orange).

8. Here is a foot: Make a 1½" bubble and 1" bear ear.

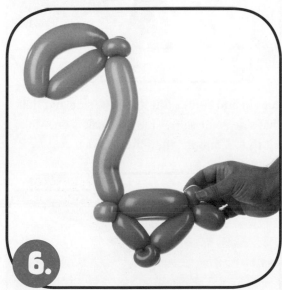

9. And then one long leg: Make a 3" to 4" bubble.

4. We will add a couple of bear ears on the bottom so we can attach the legs later: Make a 1" bear ear, 1" bear ear twist, and 2" bubble.

10. These next bear ears are a knee joint, but since our flamingo is going to be standing up, we need the balloon to go into the double bear ears and back out again straight—similar to what you look like when standing. You can see your knee, but your legs are straight. Though I doubt your legs are this skinny . . . or orange. Make a 1" bear ear, 1" bear ear, and 3" to 4" bubble. Twist the end of this bubble into the double bear ears at the bottom of the pink balloon so that the orange balloon enters vertically and leaves the same direction as the beak at about a 45-degree angle.

11. This next leg is going to be up in the classic flamingo pose—the animal pose, not the dancing one (that would be *flamenco*). Make a 3 to 4" bubble, 1" bear ear twist (for the other knee), and 3" to 4" bubble. Twist this bubble back into the double bear ears we made on the orange balloon earlier. Make sure the balloon

11.

goes in and comes out the same side and that that side is the same side the beak is on. Make a 1 to 1½" bubble, then break away.

Did you spot the inaccuracies, the dropped detail? Pink flamingo beaks have a prominent black end. We ignored this completely. Also, the second knee joint of the leg that bends up is backward—the leg actually bends the other way. The lack of these details isn't significant enough to make the design not look like a flamingo, and not including them makes the design much easier to build.

The Seahorse

When dealing with balloons, you can think in terms of line or shape. You can treat the balloons themselves as lines and your designs are basically like a connect-the-dot puzzle (although many times it is a 3-D connect-the-dot). To do this you need to figure out how to get the line to go from one dot to the next to create the shape. In most cases this is the approach I take when thinking a design through, at least with small designs. My mentor and brother-in-law tends to think more in terms of shape. How do you connect the balloons to fill up the space needed to make a necessary shape? Here your balloons are more like brush strokes coloring in an area rather than outlining it. I do this more when building large multi-balloon designs, but Paco has a knack for doing it even on a small scale. Either method works fine. Choose whatever is more intuitive to you. If, however, you can learn to see it both ways, you will have a good designing advantage.

This design is almost a combination of the two. The way the head is made, the fin, and the tail are all very linear. The balloons are used like lines in a picture. The body concentrates more on shape—the balloons together fill a shape rather than just outlining a shape.

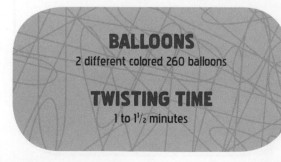

BALLOONS
2 different colored 260 balloons

TWISTING TIME
1 to 1½ minutes

1. Let's start with the head. Inflate the 1st balloon (the lighter of the two colors). Make a 1" end twist, 1" bear ear twist, 2" bubble, and 1½" × 1½" multi-twist.

2. The head isn't finished—we need to add the other balloon to complete it. Inflate the 2nd balloon (the darker of the two colors). Tie the knot of this balloon into the middle twist created by the multi-twist of the first balloon,

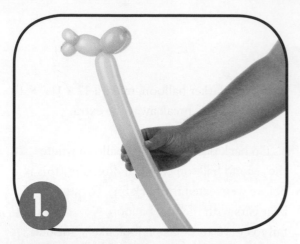

1.

2.

then go down and create a 1½" bubble on both the 1st and 2nd balloons and twist them together. This gives the back of the head a triangular shape.

3. We have a head, so let's start on the body by making some bear ears on the darker balloon. These will help stabilize the design. Make a 1" bear ear, 1" bear ear on the darker balloon, and then 1½" bubble on both the 1st and 2nd balloon, and twist together.

4. Then again on the darker balloon, we'll make some bear ears. The back fin will eventually connect here. Make a 1" bear ear, 1" bear ear, then a 2" bubble on both the 1st and 2nd balloon, and twist together.

5. Make a 2" bubble on the darker balloon, twisted back up into the last set of bear ears. The body is done. Use those bear ear hinges we made to curve the body slightly.

6. Now let's put a fin on the seahorse's back.

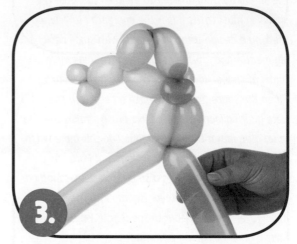

3.

4.

Using the darker balloon, make a 1" × 1½" × 1" multi-twist and break away the extra.

7. Go back down to the 1st balloon where the second balloon changed direction (this is before we created the back fin). Create two 1" bear ears with the first balloon. Now shape the tail to curve and make it look like a finished seahorse.

Just for Fun

When you finish the design hold it out in one hand and hold out your other, empty, hand. Ask the child if they would rather have the "sea horse" or the "no see horse."

The Helicopter

Here is an example of an almost purely linear design. The shapes the balloons create are pretty open, and the balloons are treated like lines that go along the outside of the shape rather than being the shape themselves.

BALLOONS
2 green 260 balloons
1 black 160 or 260 balloon

TWISTING TIME
2 to 2½ minutes

1. Let's start with the body of the helicopter. Inflate the 1st balloon (green).

2. The bottom of the front: Make a 1" end twist, 3" bubble, and 1" bear ear.

3. One of the sides: Make a 3" bubble.

4. The top: Make a 2" bubble.

5. The other side: Make a 3" bubble twisted back into the original end twist.

6. Now let's make the bottom of the helicopter. Make a 4" bubble, 1" bear ear, 1" bear ear

5.

(the tail of the helicopter will twist in here), 4" bubble twisted back into the bear ear at the

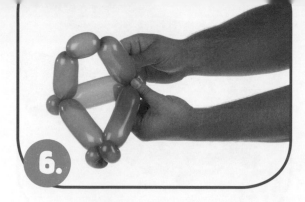

7. Next we will make the three blades. (We'll attach them later.) Inflate the 2nd balloon (black). Make a ½" end twist, 4" bubble, ½" bear ear, 4" bubble, and ½" bear ear and break away, leaving the rest inflated.

8. With your new section of balloon, make a ½" end bubble, then a 4" bubble twisted into the 1st bear ear of the first section of the 2nd balloon (the middle of the other two blades).

9. Situate the blades (all the sections that have 1" end twists or bear ears) so there is a 33-degree angle between each. The shaft should be perpendicular to the blades.

10. We'll start with the tail of the helicopter and then finish the body. Inflate the 3rd balloon (green). Make a 1" end twist, 1½" bubble, 1" bear ear, 1½" bubble, 1" bear ear, 1½" bubble twisted into the original end twist, and 1" bear ear.

11. Then the tail comes up and attaches into the body of the helicopter: Make a 4" bubble

front/bottom of the helicopter (not the end twist) and break away the extra. Now we have the square-ish front panel of the helicopter and the triangular bottom.

twisted into the back of the helicopter. This would be the bear ear pair at the bottom of the "V" shape in the first balloon.

12. Now we need to finish the upper back of the helicopter and attach the blades: Make a 3" bubble twisted into one of the twists between the 3" and 2" bubble on the front/top of the helicopter (choose one, it doesn't matter which side of the 2" bubble you connect to).

13. Take the 2nd balloon (black) and set the blades just slightly above the 2" bubble on the first balloon. We will be wrapping the 3rd balloon around the shaft that the blades rest on.

14. Make a 3" bubble twisted into the next connection on the front/top of the helicopter that is between the 2" and 3" bubbles. Make sure it goes around the shaft of the blades (the black balloon) to hold the helicopter blades in place.

15. Make a 3" bubble back to the rear of the helicopter (that same bear ear pair at the bottom of the "V" shape that the tail connected into), and break away the extra.

16. Tie the shaft of the chopper blades into that same bear ear pair and break away. Make it as long as necessary for it to be straight (probably about 2" to 3").

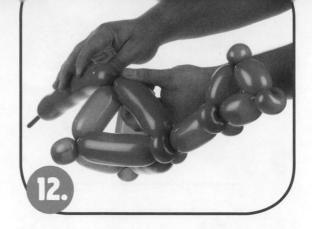

Just for Fun

As you hand the helicopter over, let the recipient know that the military often pays millions for each helicopter they purchase, but the child can have it for a measly $100,000. If the child pays up, great; if not, don't make him wait too long before handing it over.

I won't provide you with a shape-based design. Like I said, in general I prefer to treat the balloons as lines for most of my designs. But I would like to see if you can think of one yourself. Don't just outline the shape of a helicopter, but rather fill that shape with your balloons.

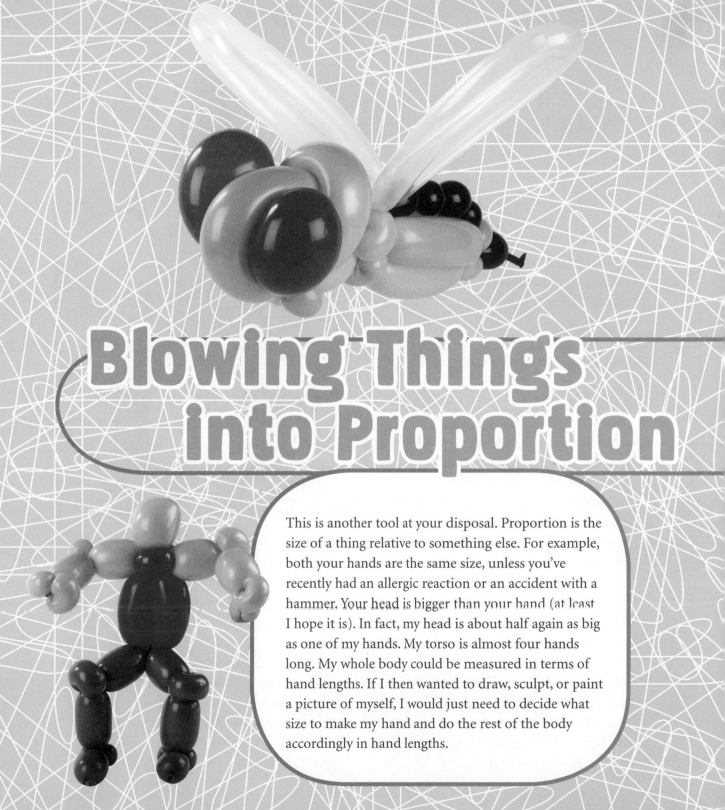

Blowing Things into Proportion

This is another tool at your disposal. Proportion is the size of a thing relative to something else. For example, both your hands are the same size, unless you've recently had an allergic reaction or an accident with a hammer. Your head is bigger than your hand (at least I hope it is). In fact, my head is about half again as big as one of my hands. My torso is almost four hands long. My whole body could be measured in terms of hand lengths. If I then wanted to draw, sculpt, or paint a picture of myself, I would just need to decide what size to make my hand and do the rest of the body accordingly in hand lengths.

You can do the same when designing a balloon sculpture. Once you know the shapes you can figure out how big each of the shapes should be compared to each other. This is another thing some people do intuitively, but not quite as many people can do it as naturally as breaking down the shapes themselves.

There are three methods I find the easiest for those who are having problems with getting things the right size.

1. If you are designing from a saved or scanned picture, you can print the picture on a grid. Draw the grid using your favorite graphics software or draw it out on a piece of paper and print the picture over it. Use the grid squares to tell you how the different shapes relate in size and transfer that to your design. If the leg of your subject fills two squares and the head fills one, make the legs twice as big as the head.

2. If you are designing from a photograph that you'd rather not draw on, try using a piece of string. Use that string to measure one part of the photo, like a leg, and then use that as your constant. How many leg lengths is the body? The head? Remember that you don't have to measure everything, just those shapes you've decided to use in your design.

3. What if the object isn't a picture? Perhaps you are looking out the window at a strange man crouching on the street. You might not want to go right up to him with a piece of string, but from a safe distance (you can be the judge of that), you still might be able to learn a few things. Close one eye. Then try extending your arm so that there is no bend in the elbow. With your fist pointing at the subject, give him a thumbs up. Always keep the elbow strait but feel free to move the thumb sideways or whichever way you need to measure the shapes in relation to it. A leg may be a thumb length while the head is a quarter thumb length. If at any time the strange man notices you and starts coming your way, I would stop. It may look like you are pointing at him or winking at him, and it is never a good idea to be rude to a strange man, especially one with a curly mustache.

Proportion doesn't stop there. Sometimes you will actually want things to be disproportionate. Our minds associate certain things with certain proportions. If we see an animal that has a larger-than-normal head and large eyes, we tend to think of it as a baby animal. A small head with a large torso tends to make us think two things—either very strong . . . or somewhat lacking in intelligence.

At this point you don't have to faithfully recreate whatever you are designing from. As an artist you can make it your own. Just remember, a true artist does it from choice, not from lack of skill. Practice until you can do it with some exactness and then decide what you want to do with it.

Balloon Sizes

This is a great time to explain balloon sizes. We've been using 260 and 160 balloons so far. It is easy enough to see that a 160 is smaller in diameter than a 260, but there is a little more we can learn about size relation. For the

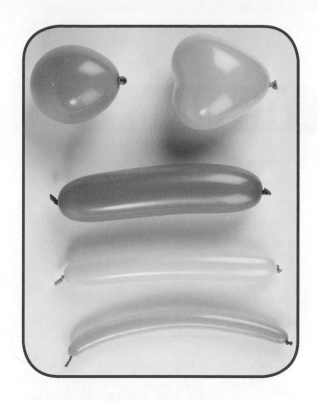

tube-shaped balloons, the first number (the "2" in "260") refers to the inflated diameter size in inches. The last two numbers (the "60" in "260") refer to the inflated length. So a 260 should pump up to be 60" long and 2" in diameter. A 160 should pump up to be 60" long but only have a 1" diameter. These are approximate measurements, however. I've found some 260s pump up slightly bigger than others. There are other sizes not used in this book, namely 350s and 646s. If you choose to work with these sizes, keep in mind that it's harder to create small designs with 3" or 6" diameters.

The tubes are not the only balloons we have for twisting. There are heart shapes, flower shaped geodes, and rounds, and Betallatex has a large line of really unusual shapes, all ready to be twisted by your creativity.

The Man

Remember that strange man out on the street? Let's go ahead and try to make him.

A human shape is one of the most useful designs. Once you know it, you can add details to make super-heroes, sports stars, soldiers—basically anyone human (or even mostly human). In this case we are going to turn a picture of me into a simple man (no jokes about my intelligence, please). To help you learn proportion, I won't be giving you the bubble sizes.

BALLOONS
1 light brown 260 balloon
1 red 260 balloon
1 blush-colored 260 balloon

TWISTING TIME
About 1 minute

1. We will make a leg first. Inflate the 1st balloon (light brown). Make a bubble for the foot, bear ear for the ankle, bubble for the shin area of the leg, bear ear for the knee, another bubble for the thigh, and bear ear for the backside.

2. Now we will create the other leg like we did the first, just in reversed order: Make a bubble for the thigh, bear ear for the knee, bubble for the shin, bear ear for the ankle, and bubble for the foot.

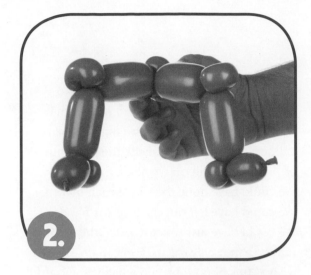

2.

7.

4.

arms later. Create another bubble the same length as the first and twist it back into the "bum" (there's that extra thickness for the body). Break away all the rest.

5. We now have legs and a torso, but we still need those arms and that head. Inflate the 3rd balloon (blush). For the hands, make two bubbles: first an end twist and then a bear ear. Make a bubble for the forearm, bear ear for the elbow, and bubble for the upper arm.

6. Make a fold twist for the head to give it a circular shape. Twist that fold twist into the two bear ears on the top of the torso to connect it to the body.

3. We now have his legs, so let's do his torso. Inflate the 2nd balloon (red). Tie the knot into the "backside" bear ear on the legs.

4. We need a little extra width to this body, so create a bubble to be one side of the body (we'll add more thickness later). Add a couple of bear ears so we can add a head and some

7. Now we need the other arm. We'll work backwards from what we did for the first arm. Make a bubble for the upper arm, bear ear for the elbow, bubble for the forearm.

8. Make two bear ears for the hand. Break away the extra.

You should have a figure of a man—hopefully a fairly proportionate man. Though, if the balloon version looks like it has lost a few pounds, I don't mind.

Again, you may have noticed we left out a few details. No hat, no hair, no curly mustache.

What details to add or leave off are up to you when designing. This design could have been made simpler yet by leaving out the red balloon. We could have made the torso out of the brown balloon we made the legs from. We could have done the whole man brown. We could have left out the bear ear hands. We could have just pinch-twisted the elbows rather than use bear ears. You can do as you wish at this point—just do whatever you think looks the best in the time you have to make the design.

How much does proportion really matter? If you had made the head on the man too big, it might not be as accurate, but everyone would still know it was a man, right? (In fact, if we were thinking metaphorically, it might even be more accurate). In some cases it is true that proportions don't make the man, so to speak, but it makes sense that you as the artist be the one to choose when things will be out of proportion. There are times when it can make all the difference. Take the case of the dolphin and the swordfish. Living in the ocean and being built for speed, the two animals have some very similar characteristics, so a lot of the detail and shapes will be the same. Their proportions, however, are very different.

The Dolphin and the Swordfish

Dolphin

BALLOONS

2 differently colored 260 balloons

TWISTING TIME

Depends on which one you do. 1 to 2 minutes should cover it, though.

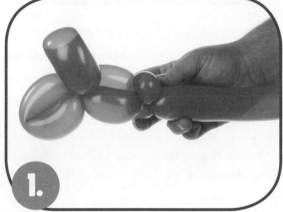

1.

1. We'll start by making the tail. Inflate the 1st balloon. Make a 1" end twist, 1" bear ear, 1½" bubble, 4" fold twist, 4" fold twist, and 1½" bubble twisted back into the bear ears then continuing on.

2. This next part won't look like much, but eventually it will become the top part of the

body. Make a 3" bubble, 1" bear ear (the top fin will eventually be connected here), and 1" bear ear. Squeeze the rest of the balloon so it has no uninflated parts.

3. We'll make the bottom of the dolphin now. Inflate the 2nd balloon. Make a 2½" bubble twisted into the end twist/bear ear combination

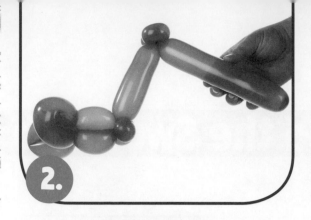

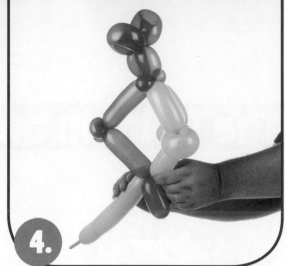

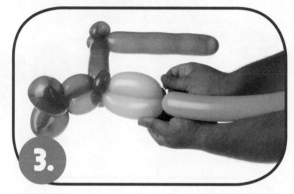

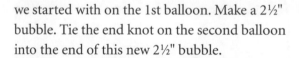

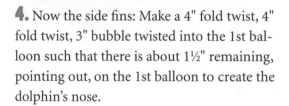

we started with on the 1st balloon. Make a 2½" bubble. Tie the end knot on the second balloon into the end of this new 2½" bubble.

4. Now the side fins: Make a 4" fold twist, 4" fold twist, 3" bubble twisted into the 1st balloon such that there is about 1½" remaining, pointing out, on the 1st balloon to create the dolphin's nose.

5. Make a 3" bubble twisted back into the two fold twist fins we just did. Make a 1" bubble twisted into the double bear ears of the 1st balloon, the ones not near the tail. Make a 3" fold twist for the top fin. Break away any extra.

6. Shape the 1st balloon between the bear ears and the end 1½" bubble to become the dolphin's "forehead."

You now have a dolphin. Let's see how different the swordfish is.

Swordfish

1. We start much the same way by making the tail. Inflate the 1st balloon. Make a 1" end twist, 1" bear ear, and 1½" bubble.

2. Here the tail is slightly different in shape: Make a 2" × 1" multi-twist, 2" × 1" multi-twist, and 1½" bubble twisted back into the bear ears.

3. Then continue on to make the top of the body: Make a 2" bubble, 1" bear ear (again, for the top fin connection later on), and 1" bear ear. Squeeze the rest of the balloon so it has no uninflated parts.

4. We'll make the bottom of the swordfish now. Inflate the 2nd balloon. Make a 2" bubble twisted into the end twist/bear ear combination we started with on the first balloon. Make a 2" bubble. Tie the end knot on the second balloon into the end of this new 2" bubble.

5. Now the side fins, with minor detail changes from the dolphin: Make a 2" × 1" × 2" multi-twist, 2" × 1" × 2" multi-twist, and 2" bubble twisted into the 1st balloon such that the 1st balloon basically lies on top of the 2nd one. Again, we are creating the nose. If there is much more than 4" remaining on the 1st balloon, then break away.

6. Let's finish up with the 2nd balloon. Make a 2" bubble twisted back into the two multi-twist fins we recently did. Make a ½" bubble twisted into the double bear ears on the top of the fish, on the 1st balloon.

7. Now for the top fin. It too is a little bit different. Make a 1" bubble, then a 2" bubble twisted into the bear ears/end twist pair that created the start of the tail. Break away any extra.

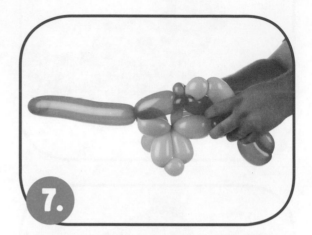

The dolphin is another Paco original and it looks pretty good. Is there a better design out there for a swordfish? I certainly hope so. That is not the point of this project. The point is that once you have a grasp and some control on correct proportions, your audience won't have to ask you if what you made is a dolphin or a swordfish. (If you want to design a better swordfish, you have enough tools to try. I suggest using a 160 for the nose.)

Just for Fun

When you pump up the first balloon, hand it over untwisted and claim it is the dolphin or swordfish. Explain that it is moving so fast through the water that it is just a big blur. When you are finished being entertained by the child giving you that look that asks, "Are you serious?" you can go back to making the design.

Remember that small balloon (the 160) that we used for the flower with the princess, for the helicopter blades, and the one I suggested after we made the swordfish? All of those were good examples of proportion. It was possible to use a 260 balloon in each of those designs, but proportionately it makes sense to have a smaller flower, thinner blades, and a thinner nose. There are many times you want a thinner balloon to help with the proportion. Here we'll be making a crocodile. If you don't have 160s yet a 260 can still be substituted—it just looks nicer having the thinner balloon for detail. We'll discuss it a little bit more after we've made the crocodile.

The Crocodile

BALLOONS
2 green 260 balloons
1 green 160 balloon

TWISTING TIME
1 minute 32¹/₂ seconds (give or take)

1. We'll start by twisting the head, specifically the upper jaw. Inflate the 1st balloon (green 260). Make a 1" end twist, 1" bear ear, 2" bubble, 1" bear ear, 1½" bubble, 1" bear ear, and 2" bubble twisted back into the end twist.

2. The lower jaw is a simple multi-twist: Make a 1½" × 1½" multi-twist.

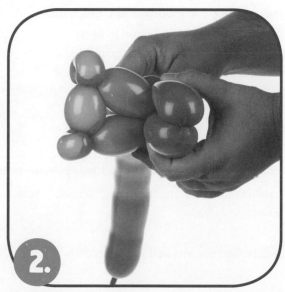

3. And then the neck: Make a 1" bubble.

4. And the first leg: Make a 2" bubble, 1" bear ear, 1" bear ear, and 2" bubble twisted back into the base of the first 2" bubble.

5. Inflate the 2nd Balloon (green 260). Tie the knot of the balloon into the base of the 2" bubbles we recently made for the first leg.

6. Now we'll make a second leg: Make a 2" bubble, 1" bear ear, 1" bear ear, and 2" bubble.

7. Put the length of the rest of the 2nd balloon against the 1st balloon and twist both together so that there is a 1" bubble at the end of the 1st balloon and the 2nd balloon is tight alongside the 1st. This is the body of the crocodile.

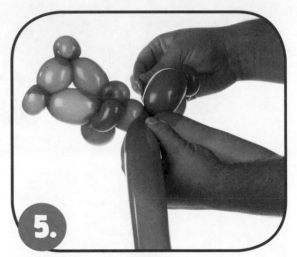

8. We still need back legs, though: Make a 2" bubble, 1" bear ear, 1" bear ear, and 2" bubble twisted back into the base of the first 2" bubble.

9. And one more leg: Make a 2" bubble, 1" bear ear, 1" bear ear, and 2" bubble twisted back into the base of the first 2" bubble. Break away any extra.

10. Inflate the 3rd balloon (green 160).

11. Let's start with some eyes: Make a ½" end twist, then a ½" bear ear. Twist these into the end twist–bear ear pair at the base of the jaw,

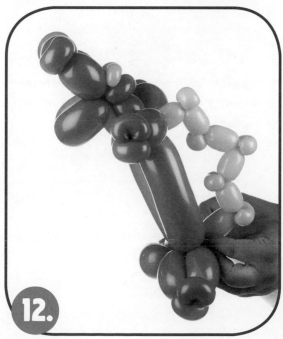

on the top of the head—much like we did when we put eyes on the snake, except we want the remainder of the 160 to go out along the neck instead of out the jaw. Make a 1" bubble twisted into the junction where the two front legs meet.

12. Now let's make some back ridges. Make a 2" bubble, ½" bear ear, 2" bubble, ½" bear ear, 2" bubble, ½" bear ear, 2" bubble, ½" bear ear, 2" bubble, and ½" bear ear. All of these should form a zigzag. If not, adjust it so they do.

13. After the last ½" bear ear on the 160 balloon, make a 2" bubble that twists into the back legs of the crocodile. Push the two bear ears on the bottom of the zigzag between the 1st and 2nd balloon that make up the body of the crocodile. This will make three ridges on the back.

14. We now have this long thin balloon pointing out where the tail should be.
Using that long thin balloon, make a 2" bubble, ½" bear ear, ½" bear ear, 2" bubble, ½" bear ear, ½" bear ear, 2" bubble, ½" bear ear, ½" bear ear, and 2" bubble.
   Break away any extra. At this point you can angle the tail at each of the bear ear pairs if you like, to give it more character.

Though I generally stick to size 260 balloons, there are certainly some exceptions. In this case I didn't want the back ridges to be as fat as the body—they should be smaller and thinner. The 160 allows me to do this. Basically anytime I want small details—a ninja's sword or a fisherman's fishing pole, for instance—I turn to the 160. There are designs that I have that only use the 160. Ladybugs and fairies are just cuter when they can be made small. The 160 is not the only other size or shape out there either. In fact, we'll play with heart balloons in just a little while.

14.

Just for Fun

Explain that this is definitely a crocodile and not an alligator. Crocodiles are easy, but in order to make an alligator you'd need a gator-aid.

We talked very briefly about some of the non-tube shaped balloons before we started making the man design. It may seem that hearts or rounds have limited potential. But it is actually because they are shaped so differently that they offer so many possibilities. Remember when we were talking about treating the balloons as lines or as a means to fill up a shape? The odd-shaped balloons are great at filling up a shape quickly, simply, and elegantly.

The Bumblebee

1. Inflate the 1st balloon (yellow). Make a 1" end twist, then a 7" fold twist (it is large enough that it is almost a loop). Push the end of the balloon through the middle of the fold twist so it creates a new large loop, one that we can actually see through the middle of.

2. Inflate the 2nd balloon (heart) so that you can just barely tell that if you kept pumping it would be heart-shaped (**see 2a**). (*See page 84 for an alternative version of the eyes using a 260 balloon.) Grab either side of the heart so the small indent is between the two hands. Your thumbs should be down where the knot

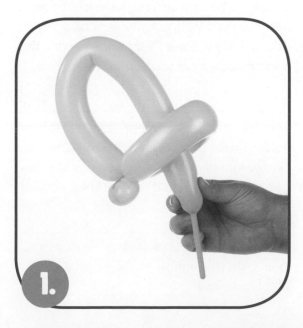

1.

2a.

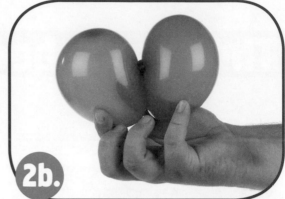

2b.

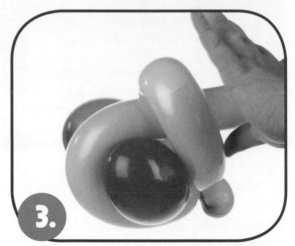

3.

is. Carefully squeeze the middle as you rotate your hands in opposite directions. You should end up with two almost pear-shaped bubbles; don't let go or they may come undone (**see 2b**).

3. Place the two bubbles inside the yellow loop of the first balloon, so that the loop goes around the twist. Then pull the end of the yellow balloon farther through the fold twist to tighten the loop around the heart. You now have bug eyes! Well, not you personally. For orientation purposes I'll let you know that the bottom of the head is where the end twist is.

4. Let's give the bee a body. Inflate the 3rd balloon (yellow). Tie the knotted end into the end bubble on the first balloon. Make a 3" bubble twisted into the 1st balloon (about 2" after it comes through the fold twist), 1" bear ear, and 1" bear ear.

5. Make a 4" bubble twisted into the 1st balloon again (the bubble on the 1st balloon should also be 4").

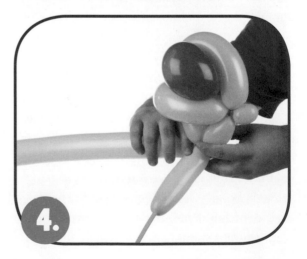

4.

bear ear, 1" bear ear (we'll attach the stinger here later), and 4" bubble twisted back up the length of the body into the bear ears near the head. Break away the end of both the 1st and 3rd balloons.

7. Arrange the three 4" bubbles so that there is one on the bottom (as the stomach) and two facing the top (as the back).

8. Time for some stripes and a stinger. Inflate the 4th balloon (black). Tie the knotted end into the first set of bear ears near the head of the bee.

9. Now we need to make the stripes along the back of the bee. Make a 1" bubble, 1" bubble, 1" bubble, and 1" bubble. These bubbles should rest in the groove created by the two 4" yellow bubbles along the back. Twist the last bubble into the rear bear ears.

10. Make a 1" bubble, then go up the balloon 3" or 4" and break away. Let it deflate to the end of the last 1" bubble we just made. Keep the 1" bubble inflated but tie the balloon at the very end of the uninflated portion to create a stinger effect.

11. Inflate the 5th balloon (clear) so only ½" remains uninflated. Tie both ends together and then push the middle of the loop to the knot

6. At this point you don't need to remember which is the 1st balloon and which is the 3rd. Use whichever seems longer. Make a 1"

and twist them to make a pair of wings (much like we did with the three loops for the princess dress).

12. Pinch-shape the end of each wing to make them more pointed. Twist the center of the wings into the double bear ears near the head of the bee. Have each wing sit on top of a bear ear to help the wings point back a little bit.

This is only one possible use of a heart balloon. A very slightly inflated heart can be used to make a fish or udders for a cow. I've seen heart balloons used to make feet with toes. In the past I've used rounds to fill in the open shapes made by linear designs. The possibilities are there for you to experiment with. Don't count them out just because they aren't tubes.

*Alternative 260 version of the eyes in case you don't have a heart. (That was not a personal judgment.)

1. Inflate the extra black 260. Make a 3" fold twist and 3" fold twist. Around the fold twists we've already made, so that they cover that "U" shape of the fold, make a 6" fold twist around one of the 3" fold twists and a 6" fold twist around the other 3" fold twist. Break away the extra.

2. Place the eyes just as was suggested with the heart balloon.

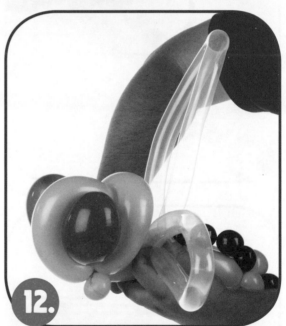

Just for Fun

Bee sure when you hand over the Bee-loon, that you emphasize all its Bee-autiful qualities while replacing the "b" in any word you say with "bee."

Coloring Your Designs

Another tool in balloon twisting that is often over-looked is color. You may think that here your choices are limited, and you'd be right, but perhaps not as lim-ited as you might imagine. Just one of the suggested brands I mentioned has well over forty different colors available in the size 260 balloon, with nearly as many offered in 160s.

There are three basic ways that the colors in your designs can affect your audience.

Contrast

Our minds try to take in the shape of the balloon as a whole, but sometimes we want the audience to see separate shapes within the design itself. Using a variety of colors can help separate the shapes. On the princess design we had one color for the dress, one for the skin, and one for the hair. If we had done the whole design blue it would have looked interesting but very, very confusing.

Perception

Colors affect us psychologically in many ways. This can vary from culture to culture. For instance, in western cultures the cool colors like purple, blue, and green are considered calming and relaxing. A "green room" is an area in a theater where the actors prepare to go onstage, and they were traditionally painted green for the color's perceived calming effect. As the name "cool" suggests, cool colors also infer a certain coldness and sometimes wetness. Warm colors like yellows, reds, and oranges are supposed to excite or agitate. This is why road signs are often warm colors. We need people to pay attention to important signs. Warm colors also suggest heat and dryness. We can use this knowledge when making animals. Do they live in warm or cool climates? Do we want them to be intimidating (black is a good color for that) or fun (try the cool colors or bright contrasting colors)?

Association

Sometimes the link between a subject and color is even stronger than what was mentioned with perception. We tend to associate certain objects with certain specific colors. When most people think of a frog they immediately think green, though we happen to know frogs come in many color patterns. When we think fish, we tend to think blue, even though there are few fish that are really blue. In fact, just like a small change in proportion can make a swordfish out of a dolphin, a small color change can make a skunk out of a cat, or a pig out of a bear. The point is that if we want people to see our simple shapes as something specific, a good color choice can point them in the right direction.

Of course, you need to realize that you will have less control over this aspect of your design than most. You will have kids that insist on having a pink bear, a purple lizard, or a red raccoon. You can try to explain your reasoning, or you can just make it using the desired colors. Trust me, it is much easier to just make it. You can influence your recipients' color choices by suggesting ones to them before ever giving them a chance to decide, but if a child

wants pink, no in-depth discourse about color theory will change her mind.

Here is a good example of the contrast principle. Skeletons are generally thought of as white, and it would make sense to make the whole balloon design white. Yet, as you will see, the ribs get a little bit lost in the design. Changing the ribs to gray helps them to stand out and separates their shape from the rest of the design.

The Skeleton

It is always good to have a few seasonal designs up your sleeve. This one has become a favorite around Halloween or the Day of the Dead. It also works well for any pirate-themed parties.

BALLOONS
3 white 260 balloons
1 gray 260 balloon

TWISTING TIME
2 minutes

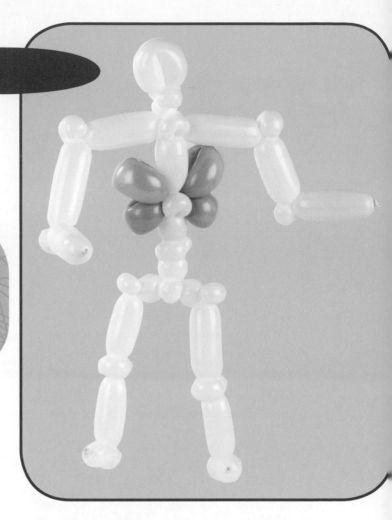

1. We'll start by making the head. Inflate the 1st balloon (white). Make a 1" end twist, 1" bear ear, and 3" fold twist.

2. Make the neck: Make a 1" bubble.

3. And one of the arms: Make a 1" bear ear, 2½" bubble, 1" bear ear, 3" bubble, 1" bear ear, and 3" bubble and break away.

4. We'll start with the second arm here. Inflate the 2nd balloon (white). Make a 3" bubble, 1" bear ear, 3" bubble, 1" bear ear, 2½" bubble, and 1" bear ear twisted into the first single bear ear on the 1st balloon (this creates the head and arms of the skeleton).

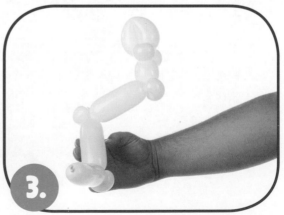

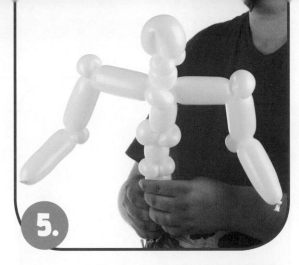

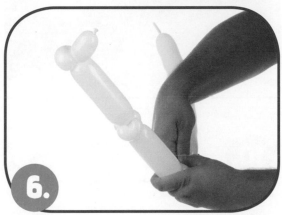

5. Now let's give our creation a spine. Make a 2½" bubble, 1" bear ear, 1" bear ear, 1" bubble, 1" bear ear, 1" bear ear, 1" bubble, 1" bear ear, and 1" bear ear and break away.

6. The skeleton could still use its legs: Inflate the 3rd balloon (white). Make a 1½" bubble, 1" bear ear, 3" bubble, 1" bear ear, 1" bear ear, and 3" bubble.

7. Hips would be nice: Make a 1" bear ear, 1" bubble twisted into the last pair of bear ears on the 2nd balloon, located at the end of our skeleton's spine, then a 1" bubble and 1" bear ear.

8. On to leg two: Make a 3" bubble, 1" bear ear, 1" bear ear, 3" bubble, 1" bear ear, 1½" bubble and break away.

9. We still need those ribs: Inflate the 4th balloon (gray). Make a 3" fold twist (just tie the knot back into the balloon), 3" fold twist, 2" fold twist, 2" fold twist and break away. You should have what looks like very small gray butterfly wings.

10. Twist the middle of all the gray "wings" into the first of the double bear ears along the spine, the ones just after the arms of the skeleton. Remember to roll it in—don't just try to push it in or you may have trouble. Do this by grabbing one half of the "wings," a small and a large wing, with your right hand while holding the skeleton and the other two "wings" with the left hand. With the middle of the gray "wings" pressed against the double bear ears, rotate or roll the wings into the bear ears as you push the balloon into the double bear ears. I hope by now it has become a habit to roll twists together.

You now have a finished skeleton with gray ribs. Pictured next to it is how it would have looked if we had used all white. Can you see how the gray immediately separates itself to become ribs? The all-white one isn't bad, but it takes a little more effort to see how it works as a skeleton.

Just for Fun

As you hand the balloon to the child, apologize that the skeleton doesn't have all 256 bones. You tried but were only able to include about 52 or so.

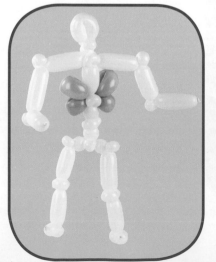

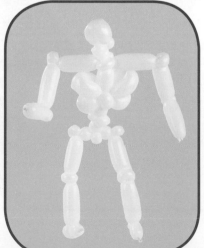

The Octopus

Here is a design that works well all one color, yet by adding some white eyes that take only seconds to make, the whole design improves considerably. I find there are very few balloon designs that aren't improved by having more than one color involved.

BALLOONS
4 orange 260 balloons
1 white 260 balloon

TWISTING TIME
45 seconds

1. Inflate the 1st and 2nd balloons (orange) so that each has only 1" to 2" uninflated on the end.

2. Place the balloons next to each other so that each of the ends are together. Fold the balloons in half but don't twist. Go down about 4" from the middle bend and twist the balloons together. You should have two 8" loops with 4 balloon ends coming out. Remember, a loop is just a fold twist that you can see through the middle of.

3. Inflate the 3rd and 4th balloons (orange) so that each has only 1" to 2" uninflated on the end.

4. This is much the same process as the 1st and 2nd balloons. Fold the balloons in half but don't twist. Go down about 3" from the middle bend and twist the balloons together. You should have two 6" fold twists with 4 balloon ends coming out.

5. Now we twist the 1st and 2nd balloons into the 3rd and 4th where all the fold twists meet. Push the two 6" fold twists, which are side by side, into the inside of the two 8" loops (**see 5a**). We should now have the body of an octopus with eight straight legs coming out. Pinch-shape twice on each leg to make them bend (**see 5b**). Right now we have a very passable octopus (**see 5c**). Few would complain if you were to hand it over, yet with a few more seconds of invested time . . .

6. Inflate the 5th balloon (white). (We really only need a few inches of white. If you have a white fragment feel free to use it.) Make a 1" end twist and a 1" bear ear and break away. Tie the end of the bubble back into the middle of the twist.

7. Tie these eyes into the area where the other four balloons meet at the fold twists.

7.

The octopus suddenly has a lot more character, and you look all the more talented. This is not simply a case of contrast. This has almost as much to do with adding on more details, like we talked about in the shapes section, but can you imagine how little it would have helped if we had made those eyes orange like the rest of the octopus? In this case it is the contrast that separates the detail and makes it worth having.

The Lion

We have talked briefly about perception and about how certain colors affect how we think about things. Let's try an experiment and learn another design at the same time.

The lion is generally considered a warm climate animal. Therefore we will make a lion using orange and brown, both of which are warm colors. At the end I will show you the same design made out of cool colors (blues) and we can see what a difference color choice can make.

BALLOONS
1 orange 260 balloon
2 light brown 260 balloons

TWISTING TIME
A little less than a minute

1. We'll start with the head. Inflate the 1st balloon (orange). Make a 2" bubble and 2" × 2" multi-twist, then tie the knot of the balloon into the middle twist created by the multi-twist. It should look just like the three-bubble group we did on the dog.

2. Let's make some ears: Make a 2" bubble, 1" bear ear, and a 1½" bubble twisted back into the first twist of the 2" bubble. We've created

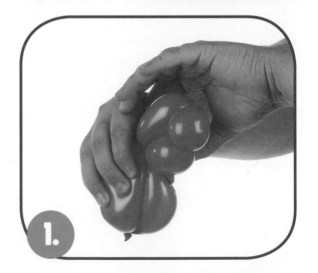

one ear. Repeat the process for the opposite ear: 2" bubble, 1" bear ear, and 1½" bubble twisted back into that first twist. Now you should have the head of a cat.

3. For the neck: Make a 1½" bubble and a 1" bear ear twist.

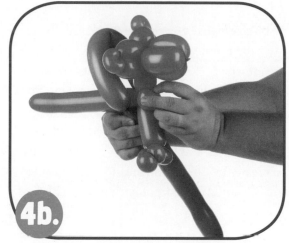

4. Next we'll make the front legs and the mane: Inflate the 2nd balloon (light brown). Make a 1" end twist, ½" × ½" × ½" multi-twist to create a foot, 2" bubble twisted into the bear ear on the orange balloon that marks the end of the neck (**see 4a**), 6" fold twist (for the mane) (**see 4b**), 2" bubble, ½" × ½" × ½" multi-twist to create the other foot, and a 1" bubble and break away. Tie the knot into the back of the foot.

5. Let's give the mane some shape. Pinch-twist along every two-thirds of the mane (you'll pinch-twist twice) to give it some shape. Push the neck of the lion just slightly into the opening of the mane.

6. Now for the back legs and the body: Inflate the 3rd balloon (light brown). Make a 1" end twist, ½" × ½" × ½" multi-twist to create a foot,

2" bubble twisted into the 1st balloon 2½" to 3" after the point where the front legs and mane are attached, 2½" to 3" bubble that follows along the body and twists into where the front legs and mane attach, 2½" to 3" bubble that twists back into where we created the third leg, 1" bear ear, 2" bubble, ½" × ½" × ½" multi-twist to create the other foot, and 1" bubble, and break away. Tie the knot back into the back of the foot.

7. Now go back to the first balloon and pinch-twist the end of it a few times to make the tail more interesting.

Now you have your lion. Let's see how it would look if we made it out of blue. It's still not bad, but it looks less like a lion. Try an experiment. Show a friend both of the pictures and tell them to choose which is the lion. If they chose the blue one, they did it just to spite me.

The Frog

Association can be a powerful thing. It is how people get logos or sayings attached to a company. It is how we decide what words are good and which are bad. In this case it can help us see a frog in a jumble of green balloons.

Again, we'll build the frog using green but show a uniquely multicolored one next to it when we finish. At that point we'll discuss when we might want to break away from traditional colors.

BALLOONS
2 green 260 balloons
1 red 260 balloon

TWISTING TIME
1½ minutes

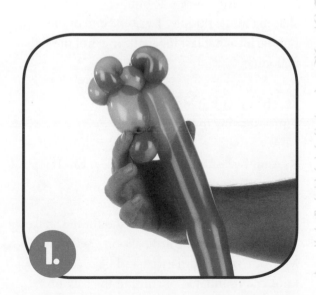

1. We'll start with the front legs, eventually using our old friend the pop twist. Inflate the 1st balloon (green). Make a 1" end twist, 2" bubble, 1" bear ear twisted 7 times, 1" bear ear twisted 7 times, 1" bubble, 1" bear ear twisted 7 times, 1" bear ear twisted 7 times, 2" bubble, and 1" bear ear.

2. Now we'll create the head between the two legs: Make a 2" bubble twisted into the end bubble, 2" bubble twisted into the last bear ear,

1.

and 2" bubble twisted into the end bubble. At this point the head highly resembles what we did for the monkey head.

3. Now we'll make the body: Make a 2" bubble, 1" bear ear, 2" bubble twisted into not the last bear ear but the one before that, then break away. It should look like a "V" with each end of the "V" attached to a side of the head. The bottom of the "V" should be a very lonely bear ear. Don't worry, he'll soon get friends.

4. Let's make the feet and back legs, starting with a foot: Inflate the 2nd balloon (green). Make a 1" end twist, and 1½" × 1½" × 1½" multi-twist.

5. Then a leg: Make a 4" bubble with a pinch-shaping in the middle. Twist the end of the bubble into that last lonely bear ear of the 1st balloon.

6. The other leg: Make a 4" bubble with a pinch-shaping in the middle.

7. And the last foot: Make a 1" bear ear, 1½" × 1½" × 1½" multi-twist, and break away.

8. We'll make eyes just as we did for the Snake (page 19): Inflate the 3rd balloon (red) only 2". Make a 1" × 1" multi-twist and tie together the knot and uninflated portion of the balloon.

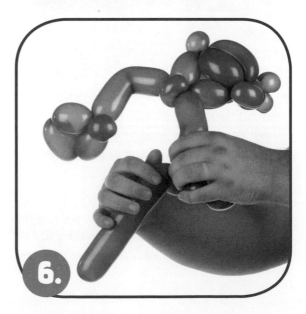

9. Pull the uninflated part of the balloon through the 2" bubbles on the head of the frog to make eyes and a tongue. Pull it through tight—we don't want dangly eyes.

10. Pop the 1" bubble between the two pairs of bear ears on the 1st balloon.

You now have a green frog. Let's look at it next to the blue and orange monstrosity. The green one registers better as a frog—but what if the child had asked for a poison arrow frog? In that case the brighter colors might have been a better choice. Of course, I think black and red would make yet an even better choice.

The Pig

How much effect does this association thing really have? When I started to write this book I had originally intended to put a bear design in. The bear was a variation of a very old tried-and-true design. When it came time to take the photographs, I made the bear pink and brown. It had a pink head and a brown body. I did not tell the people at the photo shoot what it was. The fact that it was pink made them think first of a pig. From then on they couldn't see a bear—it was always a pig. Eventually I showed them my actual design for a pig, which, honestly, has certain similarities, and decided to bring you the pig design instead. Just don't make it all brown—people might think it is a bear.

BALLOONS
2 pink 260 balloons
1 pink 160 balloon

TWISTING TIME
1½ minutes

1. Inflate the 1st Balloon. Make a 1" tulip twist (to create the nose). Remember to twist the balloon around the knot after you have it pushed in (**see 1a and 1b**).

2. Now let's make the head: Make a 3" bubble. (I find it easiest to make the rest of the following bubbles if I hold this one against my body with my palm. This way I am always holding

1a.

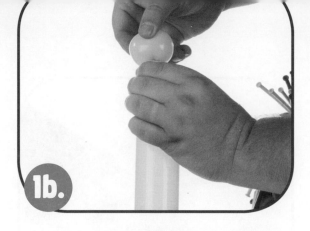

1b.

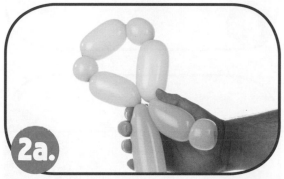

2a.

2b.

2c.

5.

one end of the balloon but both sets of fingers are free to keep twisting.) Make a 2" × 1" × 2" × 1" × 2" multi-twist (**see 2a**). Push the 3" bubble so that the end of it goes through the triangle we created (**see 2b**). Twist each of the two 1" bubbles into bear ears to keep the balloon in place. The nose should just be poking through. (You now have your pig head with the ears and nose) (**see 2c**).

3. Inflate the 2nd balloon and tie it to the bottom of the head.

4. Make a 3" × 1" × 1" × 3" multi-twist to create the front legs. This is similar to how we created the arms on the monkey design.

5. Make a 3" bubble twisted into a 3" length of the 1st balloon. This will help give some girth to the body of the pig.

6. At this point use whichever balloon is longer—1st or 2nd. Make a 3" × 1" × 1" × 3" multi-twist to create the back legs. Make a 3" bubble twisted back up into where the head meets the front legs. Make a 3" bubble twisted into the rearmost twist. The body should look like the dog's head, only with four bubbles instead of three. Well, that and the legs sticking out of it.

7. Form two 1" bubbles out what is left of your 1st and 2nd balloon and then break away both.

8. Inflate the 3rd balloon (the 160). Make a 1" end bubble that gets twisted into those two 1" bubbles we just made. Shape about 2" to 3" of the 160 balloon to be curly like we did on the snake. Pinch-shape it a few times to make sure it has a good curl. Break away the rest.

Can you see the bear in the face? How about in context of the original bear pictured below? Color has a powerful effect on how we perceive things; knowing this gives you power. (Not too much power, though. Don't let it go to your head.)

The Twister's Enemy: Time

We've touched a few times on how much time affects what you can and can't do with balloons. Many twisters decide that this means you always need to keep designs as simple as possible. It is true—simpler is faster. But with practice, good technique, and a few tricks, you can learn to tie complex balloons about as fast as other twisters are tying the simple ones.

Here are my general rules for quick twisting:

1. You are always slow at a design the first ten times you twist it. Don't judge how quickly you can tie it until you've done it at least ten times—without looking at the directions (that would be that "practice" thing).

2. Body position matters: Twist with your elbows in. Use your wrists, not your whole arms, to twist. Get used to using one hand to hold everything while the other twists (your body is great for stabilizing). Try a few of these methods, and then do what is comfortable.

3. Have degrees of complexity in designs. The swan you make at a fair should not be as complex as the one you make as a centerpiece at someone's wedding. Each of these audiences is expecting something very different.

4. The break away technique will save you time. Tie off and use those extra fragments, and you won't have to blow up a new balloon.

5. Have the right setup. Your apron and your pump will affect how quickly you can twist balloons. Find a setup that is efficient for you.

There are many more tricks out there. Some don't seem to help me with my style of twisting. I listed the ones that help me the most,

but I am sure you will find a few tricks of your own. Maybe you have already found a few.

Perhaps one of the best ways to ensure you have enough time to make a design is to have two or three designs for the same animal or object. Don't physically twist all three at one event. Having two or three designs gives you options of different complexity for different situations. In this case, we are going to learn a design for a mouse, then we'll learn a mouse, and, finally, to illustrate the point more fully, we will finish with a mouse.

The (Simple) Mouse

This is not my design. I have seen it in so many books and through so many twisters that I honestly can't find its origins. Perhaps it harks back to those simpler days of entrail balloons. If so, I don't intend to look that hard.

BALLOONS
1 gray 260 balloon

TWISTING TIME
10 seconds or less with practice

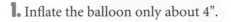

1. Inflate the balloon only about 4".

2. Here's the head: Make a 1" bubble, 1" bear ear, and 1" bear ear.

3. Now for a neck: Make a 1" bubble.

4. Then some legs: Make a 1" × 1" multi-twist.

5. And the body: Make a 1" bubble.

6. And the other legs: Make a 1" × 1" multi-twist. The rest should come out the back as a tail.

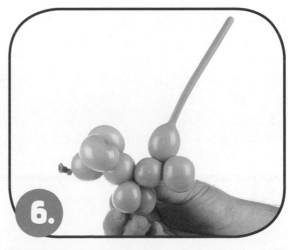

You have perhaps the simplest animal design I can think of, besides the dead and live worms we talked about earlier. Honestly, you could pump well over a hundred of these in an hour. Your wrists would be sore, but you could do it.

Simple is good, especially when it is cute, but sometimes you want to wow without taking up too much time. Let's try to figure out a medium design.

The (Medium) Mouse

Created specifically for this book, this design attempts to be somewhere between the simple version and the complex version of the mouse.

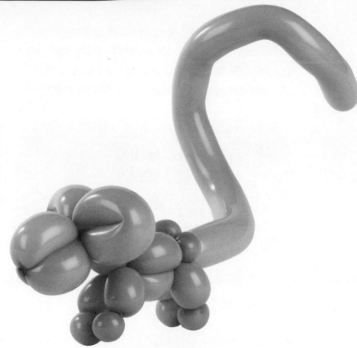

BALLOONS
2 gray 260 balloons

TWISTING TIME
About 30 seconds

1. First, the head: Inflate the 1st balloon. Make a 1½" bubble, then a 1½" × 1½" multi-twist. Tie the knot at the end of the first bubble into the middle twist of the multi-twist (much like the dog's head).

2. Then the ears: Make a 3" fold twist and a 3" fold twist.

3. Now the neck and then legs: Make a 1" bubble and a 2" × 1" × 1" × 2" multi-twist (like

1.

the monkey arms). If the rest of the balloon is much longer than 3", break the excess away.

4. Inflate the 2nd balloon. Make a 1" end twist and 1" bear ear. Twist the end of the 1st balloon into this end twist/bear ear combination.

5. Continuing with the 2nd balloon, let's make the rear legs: Make a 2" × 1" × 1" × 2" multi-twist.

6. And let's make the body more stout: Make a 3" bubble twisted up into the start of the front legs on the first balloon and a 3" bubble twisted back into the end twist/bear ear pair we started with. Pinch-shape the rest of the balloon to finish the tail.

This mouse is more complex and bigger than the simple version, though the simple version has a certain cuteness in its simplicity that this one lacks. Of course the design I like to use, if time allows, is the complex one. I think it is the cutest of the bunch. You'll see.

The (Complex) Mouse

BALLOONS
2 gray 260 balloons
1 black 260 balloon

TWISTING TIME
40 seconds to 1 minute

1. We begin much like we do with the medium mouse. First, the head: Inflate the 1st balloon (gray). Make a 1½" bubble and a 1½" × 1½" multi-twist. Tie the knot at the end of the first bubble into the middle twist of the multi-twist (much like the dog's head).

2. Then the ears: Make a 3" fold twist and 3" fold twist.

2.

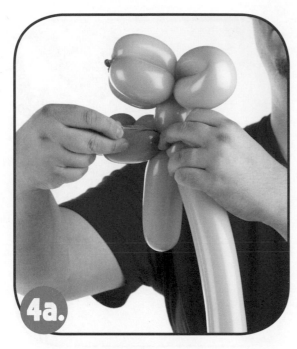

4a.

3. Now the neck and then legs: Make a 1" bubble, 1" bear ear, and 2" × 1" × 1" × 2" multi-twist (like the monkey arms). If the rest of the balloon is much longer than 3", break away the excess.

4. Let's make a different style of body. This time the mouse will be sitting up. Inflate the 2nd balloon (gray). Tie the knotted end into the bear ear by the front legs (**see 4a**). Make a 4" bubble, 1" bear ear, 1" bear ear, and 4" × 4" multi-twist and push the end of the 1st balloon between the two bubbles of the multi-twist to form the mouse's belly. Shape the rest as a tail as it comes out the back (**see 4b**).

5. Let's make little black eyes: Inflate the 3rd balloon (black). Make a 1" end twist and 1" bear ear and then break away, but don't let the other part deflate. We'll need it.

6. And now a nose: Take the fragment and tie it, then make a 1" bubble and then break away.

7. We have a bubble for the nose. It's that 1" bubble we just broke away. The rest of the black balloon can be allowed to deflate.

8. Tie the eyes into the twist (that end bubble/bear ear combination) on the 1st balloon

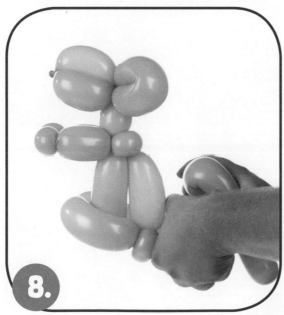

8.

where the 3" fold twists meet to make ears. Twist the nose (the 1" bubble) to the front of the face where the knot of the 1st balloon is tied to the multi-twist (like we did on the dog).

Now you have all three mice. Three latex mice. See how they run. Or float away in the wind . . .

In this case, the complex mouse does not take too much more time than the medium mouse but looks a lot better. However, I don't relish doing the complex mouse in a festival setting. The lines get long enough as it is.

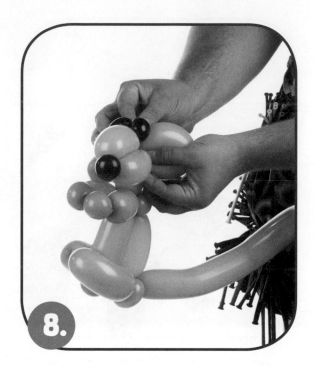

8.

Learn from Your Mistakes

It is just possible that every new design you make will turn out just like you hoped the first time. Currently I can do it about 85 percent of the time. When I first started . . . um . . . let's just say that my success rate was *slightly* less. I have an old version of a mermaid that still gives me nightmares. Yet it is hard to call even hideous mistakes unsuccessful if we are willing to use them as learning tools.

Use these general rules:

1. Don't give up on a design if it doesn't look like it will turn out. Try to finish it anyway—it might surprise you.

2. Okay, so it didn't surprise you and looks nothing like what you intended. Can you salvage part of it and tweak it into a new version of the same design?

3. That hopeless, huh? Don't throw it away in disgust. Some of my best early designs were mistakes. Does the design remind you of anything else, something completely different than what you intended? Tweak it into that new design.

4. Still not working? Hand it to some random child so you don't have to think about it anymore.

I find if I follow those general rules then I usually get something good from the experience, or a child gets a scale model of someone's small intestine. Either way, someone wins.

The "Basketball"

This design was originally supposed to be a basketball. It was hopeless as a basketball but works perfectly as something else. Let's see what you think it might be. (You'll see that in the instructions I refer to parts of it as a fish shape, but that's definitely not what it turns out to be.)

BALLOONS
2 orange 260 balloons
1 light brown 260 balloon

TWISTING TIME
30 seconds

1. Inflate the 1st balloon (orange). Bend the balloon in half so that the knot and the uninflated end of the balloon are next to each other. Twist at the halfway point and then keep the balloon bent. Halfway down, twist again. You'll have what looks like a very simple fish.

2. Inflate the 2nd balloon (orange). Repeat the process we did with the 1st balloon.

3. Place the beginning of the "tail" of one fish against the "mouth" area on the other (**see 3a**). Twist the "tail" through the "mouth" and do the same on the other end so that you get two "V"s on either end of a set of four bubbles (**see 3b**).

4. Tie each of the ends of the balloon into the opposite ends except one, preferably one with

3b.

4.

a knot. Now you should have a set of 7 bubbles with one bubble pointing out separately. I think at this point I knew it would not work as a basketball, too many indentations, which made it look like something else...

5.

5. Inflate the 3rd balloon (light brown). Make a 1" end twist. Twist the end twist onto one end of the orange contraption so that the end twist is on the outside. Make a 3" bubble. Twist the end of that 3" bubble into the other end of the orange contraption. Then tie the extra orange end to the other end.

6. Make a 2" bubble on the brown balloon, with a pinch shape halfway up. Break away the rest.

Your pumpkin is complete—just no carving, please. I still don't have a good basketball design. Usually I just make a basketball player using the general man design we figured out earlier with a small orange round in his hand. But I still use this design today as a pumpkin.

The "Monster Truck"

Another failed design is my Monster Truck. I designed it within the first few weeks of twisting balloons. Honestly, I don't have any idea how I thought it might turn out to be a truck of any kind, but I'll show you what it did turn out to be.

BALLOONS
1 green 260 balloon
1 (differently colored) 160 balloon

TWISTING TIME
Less than 1 minute

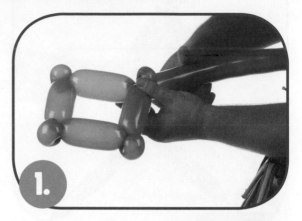

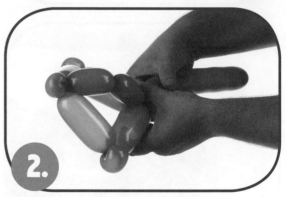

1. First I made a square: Inflate the 1st balloon (green). Make a 1" end twist, 2" bubble, 1" bear ear, 2" bubble, 1" bear ear, 2" bubble, 1" bear ear, and 2" bubble twisted back into the first end twist.

2. Then I must have thought I needed to make it less open, so I made a 1½" bubble and another 1½" bubble and twisted it into the bear ear that was diagonally across the square. We'll consider the top of the design where that diagonal is. You see where the rest of the balloon is coming out of the end twist? Pick one of the adjacent 2" bubbles to be the front. Now that we have some bearings, let's move on to the other balloon.

3. At this point I realized it wasn't going to look like a truck of any kind. From here I'll alter the design to what it eventually became. Inflate the 2nd balloon (160). Make a 3" bubble and poke it up from underneath the design through the square. Lay it perpendicularly over the front 2" green bubble so that the knot pokes out well beyond the edge of the green bubble. Hold it there while we go back to the 1st balloon.

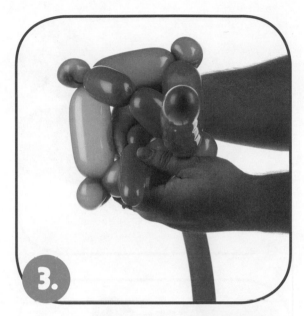

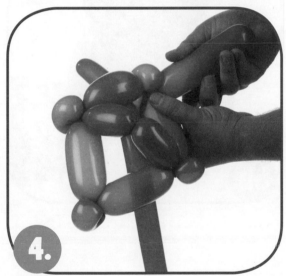

4. Create a new 2" bubble that lays across the 3" bubble in the 160 and the other 2" bubble beneath it. Twist it into the other bear ear of the front. Now the 160 pokes out between the two 2" bubbles, almost like someone sticking out their tongue between a pair of green lips.

5. Make a 1½" bubble and another 1½" bubble that gets twisted into the bear ear that was diagonally across the square. Hint: it won't be one we've already twisted a 1½" bubble into. Break away any excess.

6. Back again to that 2nd balloon (160). Create a 1" bubble that gets twisted into the bear ear (or end twist) to the right of it on the first balloon. Make a 3" fold twist back into the bear ear it came out of, and a 2" bubble that gets twisted into the next bear ear to the right (**see 6a**). Make a 3" fold twist back into that same bear ear it came out of and a 2" bubble that gets twisted into the next bear ear to the right (feel free to rotate the square as you go). Make a 3" fold twist back into that same bear ear it came out of and a 2" bubble that gets twisted into the next bear ear to the right. Make a 3" fold twist back into that same bear ear it came out of. Break away any extra you might have (**see 6b**).

Do you see what we made? We made a sorry excuse for a Monster Truck. It does however make a very cute and quick turtle. He tends to be shy. Even left alone he will slowly retreat into his shell. Actually all of him retreats, even his shell. After a few weeks' time, it's almost like he's not even there.

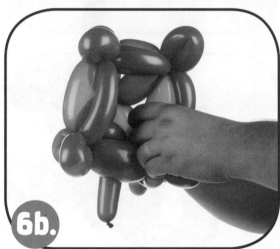

Almost Funny

Wait, that bit about the turtle was almost funny.

You may have noticed that I've tried to incorporate humor into this book. Some things may have made you smile, while other things have most likely made you groan. I will gladly accept either response. As you create your balloons for an audience, you will find that in addition to making incredible and recognizable shapes from the balloons, they also expect . . .

. . . entertainment. Perhaps you will never perform in front of people. Perhaps you will be one of those incredibly talented closet balloon artists. That's perfectly fine—just make sure it is a walk-in closet so you have room to twist.

For everyone else, here are a few pointers about using humor to twist. You'll notice that after almost every design I've given you a joke to accompany that design. Some of them are funny, some at best sound like they were *meant* to be clever. The nice thing is that as a balloon twister people expect you to be funny, and that means you don't have to try as hard; their expectations carry your jokes the rest of the way. I even tried one time to tell a joke where I knew the punch line didn't make sense but I told it with confidence. It still resulted in some small laughter, and probably a long conversation on the car ride home trying to figure it out. I am not trying to say you should attempt to be nonsensical, just that you don't have to put in too much effort to come across as funny.

Here are my general rules about entertaining:

1. Learn to relax. People will chat with you. People will like you. After all, you are making them happy by making balloons for them or their kids. You are a likable person for as long as you are making balloons. If you are relaxed, the people around you will be relaxed too. (Now turn the motivational tape over . . .)

2. Your jokes don't have to be funny. If you know you are going to pull out a groaner, just emphasize that you know it is a bad joke. This basically covers any kind of pun or elementary-school joke. Overemphasize words and hold your body in an exaggerated "ta-da" stance.

3. Keep it clean. Crude humor is easy; it is also easy to offend someone with. If your joke emphasizes a bodily function other than eating, you'll likely offend someone. Also be careful with jokes that can seem racial or prejudiced. Basically, if the joke mentions a race, nationality, hair color, or religion, avoid it.

4. You don't *have* to joke to be entertaining. Can't think of a joke? Then relay interesting facts about the subject of your design. For example, the male platypus is the only mammal with a poison gland. They have small spikes on their back feet attached to a weak poison. Not funny, but interesting and true. Quote popular movies or songs or just talk. Ask people how their day is going, how far they traveled to get there, their credit card number. . . . (okay, maybe not that last one).

This is another aspect of balloon twisting that either comes naturally or takes some practice. If you are confident in your performing abilities you needn't subject yourself to the jokes in the rest of this section. If you wouldn't mind a few more pointers and a few more designs, then keep reading.

The Horse

Let's practice with the horse. Think about the difference between a real horse and the balloon one you are making. The one you are making is much more fragile. It is a lot smaller. Depending on the color scheme, it could be a lot more colorful. Yours is filled with air. There are dozens of differences. Try to figure out some jokes that assume you think the child would treat the horse as a real horse. Of course, first, we'll teach you the design.

BALLOONS

2 light colored 260 balloons
3 dark colored 260 balloons

TWISTING TIME

1½ minutes

1. Let's start with the head: Inflate the 1st balloon (light colored). Make a 1" end twist, 1" bear ear, 2" bubble, 2" bubble, 1" bear ear, 2" bubble twisted back between the other 2" bubbles, 2" bubble twisted back into the bear ear, and 1½" × 1½" multi-twist (for the ears).

2. Now the neck: Make a 2" bubble and 1" bear ear.

3. Inflate the 2nd balloon (dark colored). Tie

the balloon into the bear ear we just made on the 1st balloon.

4. Let's give the horse a mane: Make a 1" bubble, 1" bubble, 1" bubble tied into the bear ear on the back of the head, 1" bubble, 1" bubble, and 1" bubble tied back into the bear ear where this 2nd balloon started (**see 4a**). Break away, saving the rest of the balloon. Let this new fragment deflate until only a 4" to 5" bubble remains and tie it off (**see 4b**).

5. Inflate the 3rd balloon (light colored). Tie the balloon into the last bear ear of the 1st balloon, that same bear ear we were just working with. Make a 3" × 1" × 1" × 3" multi-twist for the front legs. Run the 1st and 2nd balloon back 2½" and twist together.

6. Make a 3" × 1" × 1" × 3" multi-twist for the back legs. Make a 1" bubble and break away, tying the end back into itself. Do the 1" bubble breakaway on the 1st balloon too.

7. We'll make a tail off of what is left of the second balloon. Make a 1" end twist tied between the two 1" bubbles on the back of the horse. Make a 1" × 1" × 1" × 1" multi-twist.

8. Twist together the 2nd and 3rd 1" bubbles on the multi-twist. Break away the extra and tie it. Wrap that knot around the 2nd and 3rd

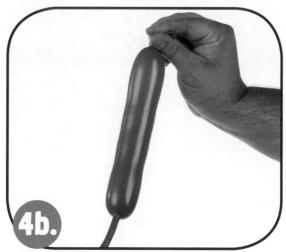

1" bubble of the multi-twist and then back into the two light colored 1" bubbles to pull the tail down against the back of the legs.

9. Leave the 4th and 5th balloons (the other two dark ones) completely uninflated—we're going to make some reins.

10. Attach one end of each balloon to the end twist and bear ear that make the mouth of the horse. Leave enough balloon on each so that they hang down a little, and then twist each uninflated balloon into the bear ears that mark the bottom of the neck and the top of the front legs. Each balloon should twist in from a different side of the horse.

Now you know the design. Did you think of any jokes? Here are a few I came up with. Remember I am doing jokes that make the assumption the kids will treat it like a real horse.

You could . . .

Tell them not to try to nail horse shoes on it—it doesn't work very well.

Tell them not to let the vet give him shots because balloon horses tend to have bad reactions.

Tell them if they intend to race it, they'd better look for the world's smallest jockey.

Tell them you knew they wanted a horse but it looks more like a Shetland pony.

Tell them, if it is colorful, you couldn't quite figure out what breed it was.

Really, the options are endless. I suggest knowing two or three jokes for each design you know how to make.

The Moose

Let's try the movie, music, and interesting fact method. Look up "moose" at your local library or online. Are there movie quotes about moose? How about songs? What interesting facts can you find? Do some thinking, and we'll see what we come up with after the moose is made.

BALLOONS
2 light brown 260 balloons
1 dark brown or black 260 balloon

TWISTING TIME
1½ minutes

1. Let's make the moose's head (the start is very similar to the pig, but without the tulip twist). Inflate the 1st balloon (light brown). Make a 3" bubble and 3" × 1" × 2" × 1" × 3" multi-twist. Twist both the 1" bubbles in the multi-twist into bear ears. Make a 1" bear ear.

2. Push the first 3" bubble through the multi-twist's center just enough so it stays but doesn't poke through the other side. Feel free to tie the knot into one of the bear ears in the multi-twist if it helps. This 3" bubble is the bottom of

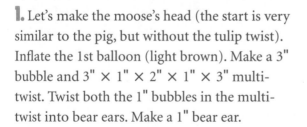
1.

the jaw, and the multi-twist is the top, with the two bear ears as nostrils.

3. Now back to the other end of the balloon. We need to finish the head and make a place for the antlers to attach. Make a 1½" bubble, 1" bear ear, and 1½" bubble twisted back into the bear ear on the back of the head. This is the head, minus the antlers.

4. Time for the body, starting with the neck. Inflate the 2nd balloon (light brown). Make a 1" end twist. About 1" down past the head on the 1st balloon, twist the end twist of the 2nd balloon in.

5. Let's make some legs (again like on the monkey): Make a 2" × 1" × 1" × 2" multi-twist.

6. Now the body: Make a 3" bubble twisted into the 1st balloon after 3" (much like we just did on the horse).

7. Now the rear legs: Make a 2" × 1" × 1" × 2" multi-twist.

8. Determine which of the 1st or 2nd balloon has the most uninflated. Twist the balloon that has the largest uninflated section back up the body to where the first legs are connected to give more heft to the body. Break away any extra.

9. With the other balloon, make a 1" bubble, if possible, for the tail and then break away the rest.

10. Antler time: Inflate the 3rd balloon (dark brown or black). Make a 1" end twist and then twist it into the bear ear on the top of the moose's head (like on the dog design). Make a 3" × 1" × 1" × 1" multi-twist. Then do the same going out the other side of the bear ear: 3" × 1" × 1" × 1" multi-twist. Break away the extra.

You now have a moose. Did you think of anything? Here is what I came up with:

You could do the *Monty Python and the Holy Grail* opening sequence: "A moose bit my sister once. No, really . . ."

Interesting fact: a moose will generally live between fifteen and twenty-five years.

Interesting fact: moose antlers can grow to be more than five feet across.

Interesting fact: moose are members of the deer family.

Interesting fact: the plural of moose is . . . moose.

Interesting fact: moose are good swimmers.

Do your best Bullwinkle impression as you hand the moose over.

The Tank

This is one of the more complicated balloon sculptures in the book, about on par with the princess. Of course, by now, nothing is daunting to you.

If the name of the sculpture itself can mean two different things, then it is fun to pretend you didn't understand which design they meant. The tank is a good example. It is a design for a military tank, but halfway through you can claim you were making an aquarium. "What, you didn't mean aquarium? And I was going to put a mermaid in it and everything . . ."

BALLOONS
2 green 260 balloons
1 black 260 balloon
1 green 160 balloon

TWISTING TIME
2 to 2½ minutes

1. Let's make the body of the tank. It is similar to the turtle design we learned earlier, except it's more rectangular than square. Inflate the 1st balloon (green 260). Make a 1" end twist, 3" bubble, 1" bear ear, 4" bubble, 1" bear ear, 3" bubble, 1" bear ear, and 4" bubble twisted back into the original end twist. Break away the extra at this point—we'll finish with another balloon.

2. Inflate the 2nd balloon (green 260). Tie the end of the balloon into the end twist of the 1st balloon (where we just left off). Make a 3" bubble and 2" bubble twisted into the bear ear diagonally across the rectangle.

3. Make a 3" bubble twisted into the bear ear along the shorter edge of the 1st balloon (you'll have two 3" bubbles next to each other).

4. Make a 2" bubble (the twist should rest right over the twist between the first 2" and 3" bubble diagonal we made). Make a 3" bubble twisted diagonally across the rectangle into the opposite bear ear and break away. We now have what vaguely looks like that turtle shell we did before, only elongated.

5. Now for the gun turret. Get ready for some really small bubbles. Inflate the 3rd balloon (green 160). Make a 1½" bubble (this would be the gun chamber—it should stick out of the rectangle we are about to make). Make a ½" bear ear, ½" bear ear, ½" bubble, ½" bear ear, 1" bubble, ½" bear ear, 2" bubble, ½" bear ear, 1" bubble, ½" bear ear, and ½" bubble twisted into the double bear ears so that it comes out into the middle of the newly formed rectangle.

6. Now we need to be able to connect the turret to the tank. When this is finished, it will look like a little capital "L." Part of the "L" should

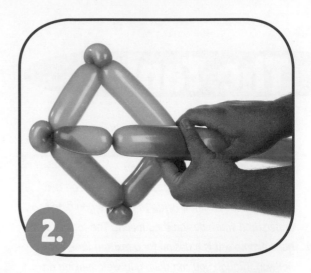

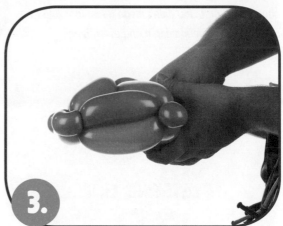

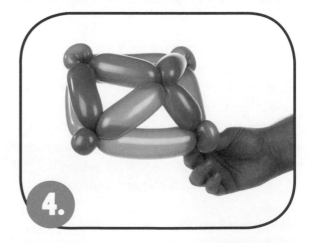

5.

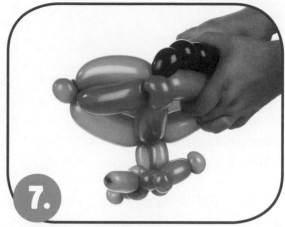

7.

6a.

6b.

be hidden within the rectangle as if it came straight back from the gun chamber. The other part should exit the rectangle perpendicular to it. Okay, here we go: Make a ¾" bubble, ½" bear ear, ¾" bubble, ½" bear ear (this is the base of the turret) **(see 6a)**, ¾" bubble twisted back up into the previous bear ear (two bear ears ago—we aren't doing a fold twist), ¾" bubble twisted back into the double bear ears, and break away. The bear ear at the base of the turret should be twisted into the 2nd balloon where the two 2" and two 3" bubbles meet **(see 6b)**.

7. Now for the treads: Inflate the 4th balloon (black). Turn the tank over so that the turret we just made is on the bottom, and so that the side of the green rectangle that has two overlapping bubbles is pointed away from you. Tie the black balloon into the corner on the left of these two overlapping green bubbles. Make a 1" bubble, 1" bubble, 1" bubble, and 1" bubble twisted into the next corner on the left (again feel free to rotate clockwise as we make the design).

8. Make a 3" bubble twisted into the next corner on the left, then a 1" bubble, 1" bubble, 1" bubble, and 1" bubble twisted into the last corner (it should be the other side of those overlapping green bubbles), and break away.

You did it. Take the time to pat yourself on the back, or you can have someone do it for you and show them your tank at the same time.

What other names of designs can you intentionally get confused?

"Is it a dog or a hot dog?"

"I'm sorry, I thought you said you were feeling horse . . ."

"Here is your unicycle—what do you mean motorcycle?"

"I made you just a bug, I didn't think it right to specify a guy or a ladybug."

"Eagle? You want an eagle? Well then, you'll have to join the Boy Scouts."

"I'm sorry, I don't know what kind of key a monk uses."

The Football and Goal Post

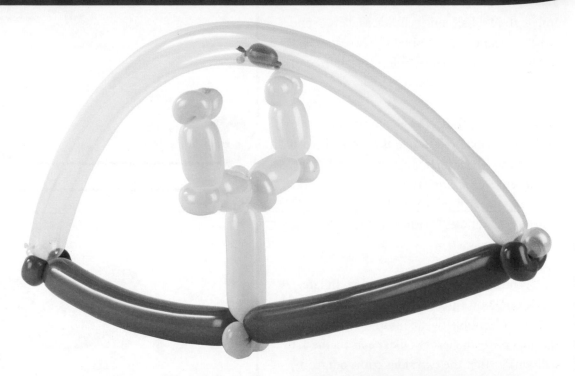

We talked a little bit about what to avoid so as not to offend people. Two other subjects to be careful with are politics and sports. Despite that, some of the most popular designs are sports related. Not too many political ones, but plenty of sports ones. How would you go about making a joke and being sure not to offend your audience? Well, let's teach you a design first.

This design features balloon stuffing again, but this time with a different colored balloon inserted.

BALLOONS
1 green 260 balloon
2 yellow 260 balloons
1 clear 260 balloon
1 light brown 160 balloon

TWISTING TIME
40 seconds to 1 minute

1. Let's make the first half of the goalpost. Inflate the 1st balloon (yellow). Make a 1" end twist, 1" bear ear, 2" bubble, 1" bear ear, 2" bubble, 1" bear ear, 3" bubble, 1" bear ear, and 1" bear ear and break away.

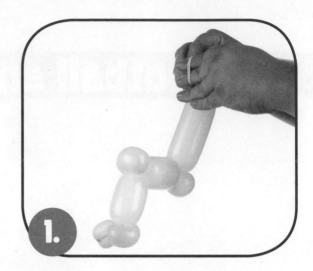

2. Now we can finish the goal post: Inflate the 2nd balloon (yellow). Make a 1" end twist twisted into the last single (not double) bear ear on the 1st balloon (the single bear ear connected to the 3" bubble). Make a 2" bubble, 1" bear ear, 2" bubble, 1" bear ear, and 1" bear ear and break away.

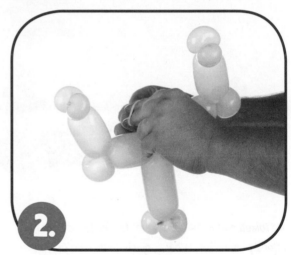

3. A little bit of the field comes next: Inflate the 3rd balloon (green). Make a 1" end twist, 1" bear ear, 6" bubble twisted into the bottom of the goal post (the last two bear ears on the 1st balloon) so that the two sides come out from the goalpost in opposite directions. Make a 6" bubble, 1" bear ear, and 1" bear ear and break away.

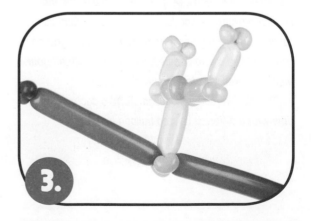

4. Inflate the 4th balloon (light brown). Make a 1½" bubble and break away (we are making a tiny football to go inside the clear balloon. If you have a fragment and want to use it you'll waste less balloons).

5. Inflate the 5th balloon (clear). Place the tiny football on the knotted edge of the clear balloon (**see 5a**). Hold the clear balloon with your

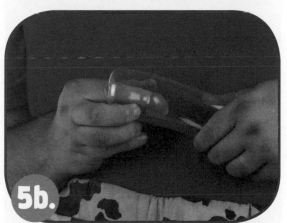

left hand, and with your right hand place your pointer finger over the tiny football, holding it against the clear balloon. Your thumb and middle finger should be on either side of the football to stabilize it as you stuff the balloon. Now stuff the balloon (**see 5b**). The football may be a little harder to control than the bubble for the jet was, so just make sure it can't escape off to the side. Once the football is inside and you've broken away (**see 5c**), tie the clear balloon off and we'll start twisting it (**see 5d**).

6. Make a 1" end twist (make sure the football isn't inside it) and twist this into one of the pairs of bear ears on the 3rd balloon. At the other end of the clear balloon, twist the last inch into the other set of bear ears on the 3rd balloon. Again, be careful that the football doesn't end up inside of it. Move the now curved clear balloon so that it goes between the two posts on the goalpost.

What kinds of jokes did you think of? If it is a small crowd, you could find out who the rival team is before saying anything. Then you say the coach of the rival team uses this balloon as a diagram to help his players understand what a field goal is, but it doesn't seem to be helping.

Better yet, use the design to praise their favorite team or player. Ask how does [insert hero here] kick their field goals? Like this! And then move the football from one end to the other. Of course, [insert hero here] rarely has to kick a field goal—they're always making touchdowns!

6.

General Information

Remember that section I told you about at the beginning of the book? The one that gives you all sorts of useful information, but one that can seem a little . . . mundane . . . when you are starting and excited to learn the art that is balloon twisting? It's here. Please don't close the book. This stuff is important. I promise. We'll discuss everything from pump selection to balloon storage. Having the right equipment is important—it doesn't matter how well you can make a princess if your pump breaks, or how cool your tank is if your balloons keep popping.

Balloon Pumps

There are a myriad of choices out there as far as pumps go, but they generally break down like this (that was perhaps a bad choice of words):

Squeezable Hand Pumps

Made to fit in the palm of your hand, these pumps are light and small and virtually indestructible. Since it takes about 20 pumps to fill a balloon, though, your hand will likely feel destroyed after about 2 to 3 balloon animals.

Standard Party Pumps

These vary from very cheap plastic pumps (that usually come with a balloon instruction book) that may or may not work when you take them out of their packaging, to the decent quality pumps that can be found at most party stores that sell balloons. The decent quality pumps endure about 8 hours of use before the neck of the pump breaks off. It takes about 4 pumps to fill a balloon.

Good Quality Hand Pumps

I endorse these heartily. These pumps can be taken apart and cleaned, and they are a decent size, though not pocket-sized. The lack of pocket-sizedness rarely matters if you have a good balloon apron. We'll talk about aprons later. And they last. I finally replaced a set after about 4 years of continuous use. They had not broken down but were so badly sun-bleached

that they no longer looked attractive. This pump also takes 3 to 4 pumps to fill a balloon.

Spaghetti Pump

This is a good quality small hand pump made specifically to inflate 160s. The quality is as good as the good quality hand pumps above, but you can't use them for anything but 160s—it would take too long to inflate anything larger. If you find it hard to get 160s to fit on a larger pump, this would be a good second pump to have.

Large Festival Pumps

Good for your county fair or festival situation, these pumps stand upright on the ground and one pump is enough to fill a balloon. They too last a long time, just don't expect them to be too mobile. They are great when stationary but are a bit awkward to move from place to place.

Mobile Motorized Pumps

These really vary. Some are quiet, some are noisy. Some pump up the balloons great, others struggle. Some heat up quick, others stay cool relatively well. Some burn right through their batteries, others will give you a few hours. In the end even a good one will start to feel heavy after a couple of hours of standing. If you are really concerned about the weariness of pumping then do a little research and find one right for you. I personally prefer the hand pump.

Large Motorized Pumps

These are the heavier, non-battery powered pumps. They too can vary greatly in quality and they take a little getting used to. I would not recommend them for the type of work presented in this book, but if you ever decide to do designs requiring hundreds to thousands of balloons, this may be the way to go. (Don't try to do designs using hundreds to thousands of balloons in a festival setting—the line tends to get unruly.)

An additional note on good quality hand pumps:

Since these are by far my favorite multi-use pump, I thought I would provide a little more detail. These pumps are recognizable by the fact that they can be taken apart (and also put back together) and by the small ridges that encompass the body of the pump. For those with larger hands I suggest the blue-and-grey version that can be purchased at Tmyers.com. The handle can be uncomfortable in smaller hands but is just about right for larger ones and it takes fewer pumps to fill a balloon, which can add up later on. For those with petite hands, I suggest Qualatex's purple and pink version. It has a narrower handle and a tapered edge to the nozzle, making it easier to get the small 160 balloons on. Both are nigh indestructible—just don't let a toddler get a hold of it. Honestly, toddlers are up for those kind of challenges.

Aprons

We've talked about ways of doing balloons faster and being more efficient in how you hold the balloons. One of the best ways

is by using a good balloon apron. I prefer to design my own, though inevitably someone else sews them. My talent lies in sculpting, not tailoring. Here are a few apron ideas.

The Server's Apron

This is the kind of apron restaurant servers wear. It usually fits around the waist and has two large pockets, and perhaps a pocket for tips as well. The advantages are you don't have to sew anything, it is relatively cheap, and you can use it right away. The disadvantages are that you can't separate colors to make them easy to find, and the apron doesn't do well to show off your uninflated balloons since they are all hiding in the big pockets. If you let the balloons show they will most likely fall out of this type of apron.

Belt Apron

This is the style I use. It is custom-made and designed, though anyone who sews one will

tell you it is a pain to sew. They do sell pre-made belt aprons that aren't too expensive, but they never seem to be able to hold enough balloons for my taste, or they aren't organized the way I would like them to be. So the advantages of a custom-made belt apron are clear organization of your balloon supply and visual appeal. The disadvantages include the time it takes to design it and the possibility of losing the friendship of whomever you ask to sew it for you.

Modified Kitchen Apron

This apron involves taking a kitchen apron of your choice and sewing pockets onto it. I know a couple of friends who use this type of apron and like it well. The advantages are that it makes it easier to sew while keeping customization. Depending on the pocket style, it may or may not show the uninflated balloons, and it has better weight distribution than the belt varieties. Disadvantages include having higher pockets, which can get a little awkward as you are reaching for balloons.

Vest Apron

Here you simply purchase a good fly fishing vest and, using Velcro, separate the balloon

colors and put them in the pockets. This is a good choice for a first apron. The advantages are that it is pre-made, relatively inexpensive, and easy to find, and the balloons can be easily organized and displayed. Disadvantages include a few pockets that are awkward to reach, and very limited color choices for the vests (though we have found pink and pastel blue ones in the past).

Accessories

There are a few accessories in the balloon-twisting world that can speed up twisting time,

make your designs more interesting, or simply make more designs possible.

The Sharpie

Have details you want to add but can't seem to do it out of balloons? Want to make the design recognizable but don't have time for the complexity it would take? The Sharpie marker can solve both of these problems. Draw faces, spots, scars—anything your artistic capabilities can handle. Just realize that once the balloon shrinks, the sharpie ink has a tendency to come off (and it's still permanent).

Bouncy Balls

Balloon stuffing not working for you? Try pushing a bouncy ball inside the balloon. Besides being heavier and rolling around easier, bouncy balls come in glow-in-the-dark versions that you can use to make designs like an angler fish with real glowing parts! (Glow sticks also work well for that endeavor.)

The Magic Pipe

Released by Qualatex, this little beauty will allow you to put anything inside of a balloon that can fit inside the pipe without it being wrapped up in the balloon itself. Engagement rings for that unique proposal, water for that squishy effect, or beads to cause a rattlesnake's tail to rattle are all possible with this device.

Accessories are really only limited by your imagination. That is not to say that if you don't use many accessories you are limited. I'm sure you're still very imaginative.

Balloon Storage

If your balloons are popping all the time, it is most likely due to either the brand of balloon

again will lessen their life. Store the balloons in some shadowed corner, or in storage bins for organizational and convenience purposes.

Mark the date on the balloon bags with a ball-point pen. This way you can use your oldest balloons first, before they get any older and frailer.

Sometimes even with all these precautions you will just get a bad bag of balloons. Know that if it is one color that keeps popping, it is not you—it's the batch.

you are using or how you are storing them. Most balloons are made from natural latex. This means they are biodegradable and nontoxic and generally friendly to the environment. This also means the longer you have them the weaker they will get. Yet under the right conditions, balloons can stay fresh for months, even years.

The first key to keeping balloons fresh is to make sure you don't buy so many that it will take you years to get through them. Buy enough to last about 2–3 months.

Next, find a cool place to store them. Excessive heat will weaken the latex quickly. Even having them in a warm place for more than a few days can significantly increase the chances of popping. I have even heard of balloon twisters storing their balloons in the refrigerator, though personally I think that would be hard to explain to visitors.

Keep the balloons out of direct sunlight. Sunlight helps oxidize the balloons, which

Twisting Environments

I have twisted in just about every environment except space (though I'm willing). I've twisted balloons in freezing snow, sweltering heat, and pouring rain. Outdoors, indoors, underground. So I have learned that there are environments that are just more friendly to balloons and twisting.

Everything that goes for storing balloons also goes while you are twisting them (though I must insist on no refrigerators at this point).

The Outside Environment

Balloon animals are indoor animals—or at least they should be. Almost anything in an outdoor environment will try to pop your creation. Trees, concrete, grass, and children are the most likely culprits. You can try to warn the children of the dangers of touching the balloon to the ground. Don't be surprised when a good percentage try it to see if you are lying by persistently hitting the ground with a look on their face that says, "See, it isn't true," until it pops. Many times those same kids will then try to cut into the front of the line to get a new balloon.

Sunny days are great for play but horrible for balloons. The oxidation rate increases as the balloons are filled, making them even weaker. Also, the balloons in your apron are effectively in an oven, getting weaker every moment. If at all possible, find some shade—it will be good for you and your balloons.

Cold and snow are miserable to twist in. Numb fingers make for slow twisting. The balloons themselves get soft and fragile when pumped up in extremely cold conditions and the snow will get the balloons wet, making them untwist more easily.

Rain, besides generally driving away crowds, will also get the balloons wet. Wet balloons are hard to twist into anything of any complexity. And the balloons left over in your apron will be covered in little dust smudges as the rain dries, making them twice as likely to pop the next time you use them.

For the above reasons I prefer to twist

balloons indoors. I say "prefer." Eighty percent of the events I am hired to do are outside. The best you can do is try to get the conditions such that you will have shade or cover as you twist, and then just be content in knowing that you are making people happy. Oh, and don't forget the sunblock.

Inflating with the Mouth

One of the most common comments I get when I use a pump is that I am cheating. I

am not sure who exactly made the rulebook and why I wasn't consulted, but it seems to be some sort of general consensus that using pumps is "cheating." Yet there are real dangers associated with blowing up this type of balloon with your mouth. Even the information on the balloon bags will tell you so. The latex is tight and thick, and the pressure needed to inflate one is great. This is why I again recommend that you use a pump and wow people with your designs instead.

Because I know there are people who will try anyway, I will give a small guide to the best way to inflate a balloon animal balloon with the smallest risk to yourself. Again, I must stress that it isn't worth it. Turn back now while you can.

Don't do this alone—make sure there is someone else in the room in case you should faint. First, you will want to weaken the balloon by stretching or inflating it beforehand with a pump and then letting the air out. Put the balloon up to your lips, holding the lipped end of the balloon with one hand and lightly pinching the balloon with your other hand right after the fingers on the first hand. Blow from your diaphragm, not from your cheeks. If your cheeks bulge out, you are doing it wrong and it can be dangerous. You should be pushing the air up from your stomach. As you blow, pull gently on the balloon near your mouth with your free hand and slowly follow the end of the inflated section as you continue to inflate the balloon. Inflate as much as you can or wish to.

Did you try it? Now do you understand? The section on pumps was just a few pages back.

In the Business of Balloons

I think the number one question I get asked while plying my trade is, "Do you do this full time?" Yes, yes I do. So can you if you really want to. I do mean really want to, because it will take a while until you can make a decent living at it. (Oh, and it requires a very understanding spouse or consigning yourself to being single).

Most people who do balloon twisting start it as a hobby. In fact, most end it as a hobby too. But perhaps you are one of those few who love it so much that you want to do it more and more. People will start to offer to pay you to do it. This section is for those who wish to make a business or side business out of your hobby. If nothing else, it can help pay for itself. Realize if you make enough money, you will need to pay some taxes on it.

Restaurants and Street Performing

The easiest way to make money is either restaurant performing or street performing. This is not the most lucrative way, just the easiest. Before you go set up on a busy street corner, though, make sure you know about your local laws. Some states require permits for street performing, and other laws may apply to our trade as well. Also make sure you don't encroach on entertainers who are already there.

Restaurants are often happy to have a balloon twister come in. Some are willing to pay for the privilege, but many are not and some won't even let you wear an "I work for tips" button. Decide what you are willing to do and give it a couple of weeks to see if it will work out.

Birthdays and Other Small Parties

Usually this will require at least a yellow page ad or a web presence. Since balloons are so visual, a website may even be the more important of the two. The way I broke into parties was by first going into a restaurant. Once the customers realized I could do more than dogs and swords, they started to ask for business cards. From there it expanded to some really good word-of-mouth, and soon birthday parties became the majority of my business.

Another option is to let local party planning or event planning companies know you are available for parties. Many of them have more shows than they have talented people to staff. They will take a booking fee, but you'll probably make more money than you would have asked for anyway.

Business and Corporate Events

This is not an easy area to break into, but it is lucrative. The first thing you have to do is figure out a way to separate yourself from the other balloon twisters out there—something unique to you or very few other balloon twisters, or something you do much better than most other balloon twisters. I tend to sell myself on my big woven designs. At this point, you might want to consider getting an agent. Once again, since he or she is booking events for you, he or she will take a piece of the pie. But since agents generally get you a bigger pie, you'll still get more than you would otherwise. If you truly want to focus on this market, arrange your website to reflect that. Also by this point you should have a contract available to secure the work and protect your interests. Require some sort of deposit—it helps keep them from backing out at the last minute after you've already turned down other shows.

Festivals and Fairs

This is not easy work, but it is a lot of hours in one place and that means less searching for work. Also during busy fair seasons, the pay can be very decent. There are a couple of ways to break into this market. One is by attending conventions where fairs are looking to hire entertainment. Another is by applying directly to the fairs themselves. Be prepared for long lines and sore fingers, though.

Conclusion

By now you should have all the tools you need to create your own designs, be entertaining, and even make some money. Don't limit yourself to the things I've given you—this is just a way to get you started. Also, don't feel discouraged if at first your designs don't come out the way you hope. My first version of a mermaid looked more like a manatee. And not even a pretty manatee.

Let's try one more thing. Pick something you really want to know how to make out of balloons and let's walk through that designing process.

First, look at pictures of that object. Do an image search online or find a photo you already have. Now figure out what shapes and details are needed to capture the essence of your subject. What twists and techniques do you know to be able to make those shapes?

Think through how to put those shapes together, remembering that bear ears make great connection points.

Are there important colors specific to your subject? Don't forget to include them.

Go ahead and try to build it. Focus on proportion.

How did it turn out? If it didn't quite work, don't forget to try to salvage something from it. Does it need just a few small changes? Is there another design lurking in those twists?

Last of all, make sure you are having fun, but don't give up if you get frustrated. Like anything else, to do this well requires patience, practice, and commitment. If at first you don't succeed, then try and try and try and try, take a lunch break, and then try and try and try again. You'll get it.

Resources

Balloons and Accessories

www.tmyers.com

Tmyers is great with both their selection and prices and carries the top two balloon brands, Qualatex and Betallatex. They carry both of the hand pumps I recommend, the one I use (called the 260 Blaster Pump) and the one my wife uses (the Qualatex 2 way hand pump). They also carry the Qualatex Magic Pipe and tons of other balloon accessories.

Stores that Carry Qualatex or Betallatex

Partyland

As of the writing of this book the Partyland franchise could be found in 18 states through the continental U.S. and in over 20 countries around the world. I'm not sure about international locations, but the U.S. locations should carry some Qualatex 260 balloons. Usually they carry the assorted color variations only.

Zurchers

This store seems to be available only in Idaho and Utah. They also carry the assorted color 260 packs from Qualatex as well as the Qualatex 2 way hand pump that my wife likes to use. (It is the pink and purple one with ridges on the base.)

General Information and Networking

www.balloonhq.com

If you want to see what other people are doing in the field, get some ideas for new designs, and learn about different aspects of balloon twisting and decorating, then you can't go wrong by visiting balloonhq.com. Many of the world's best balloon twisters are members, and it is certainly easier to search through the photos if you are a member, but you can access most of the site for free. You can even post a listing for yourself if you plan do balloons as a side job or a full-on business.

Balloon Conventions

Twist and Shout

www.balloonconvention.com

This convention changes locations and time every year to help facilitate more twisters from different areas to be able to come. Learn from some of the top balloon twisters in the world, compete against your peers, and jam in an open jam room to all hours of the night.

Diamond Jam/Balloon Camp

www.diamondjam.com

Home to the famous balloon fashion show (they make dresses out of balloons), the

Diamond Jam and subsequent Balloon Camp are well known by balloon twisters. Again, you can learn from some of the top people in the field. Participate in timed competitions or competitions based on entertainment skill. And share designs in the jam room. You can choose to go to the Diamond Jam, which focuses on balloon twisters, the Balloon Camp, which focuses on balloon decorating, or go to both. Diamond Jam/Balloon Camp is held every summer in Las Vegas.

World Balloon Convention

www.worldballoonconvention.com

Begun in 2010, this new annual event is run completely by Qualatex. It features dozens of events, including parties, competitions, classes, and even a tour of the Qualatex Plant.

Index